FAT QUARTER
TOYS

FAT QUARTER
TOYS

25 projects to make from short lengths of fabric

Susie Johns

First published 2019 by
Guild of Master Craftsman Publications Ltd
Castle Place, 166 High Street, Lewes,
East Sussex, BN7 1XU, UK

A catalogue record for this book is available from the British Library.

Publisher Jonathan Bailey
Production Jim Bulley and Jo Pallett
Senior Project Editor Sara Harper
Editor Cath Senker
Managing Art Editor Gilda Pacitti
Design & Art Direction Wayne Blades
Photographer Neal Grundy
Step Photography Susie Johns

Colour origination by GMC Reprographics

Printed and bound in China

A note on measurements
The imperial measurements in these projects are converted from metric. While every attempt has been made to ensure that they are as accurate as possible, some rounding up or down has been inevitable. For this reason, it is always best to stick to one system or the other throughout a project: do not mix metric and imperial units.

CONTENTS

INTRODUCTION

There are so many toys available in the shops for babies and young children. A whole industry is devoted to making toys that stimulate the development of body and brain. If you enjoy sewing, though, what could be better than making a beloved baby some unique, hand-made toys that are sure to become firm favourites as he or she grows and develops? People who sew tend to be resourceful, creative and thrifty. With this in mind, the toys in this book are quick and straightforward to make and none of them requires any specialist skills or expensive materials.

You don't need much in the way of fabric to create a home-made toy. Fat quarters are just the right shape and size for many projects. So what is a fat quarter? It's a clever way of cutting a yard or metre of traditional quilting cotton fabric into four pieces. If you were to cut a quarter of a yard or metre from a length of fabric, you would have a strip measuring 9in (23cm) by the width of the fabric, which is usually 44 or 45in (112 or 114cm). A fat quarter is cut in a different way: cut half a yard/metre of fabric, then cut this piece in half. This gives you a piece of fabric approximately 18 x 22in (45.5cm x 56cm). This squarish shape is very versatile. Buying fat quarters also makes it possible to buy four different fabrics for the same cost as a yard or metre of a single design.

Fat quarters are a good way of building up a collection of colours or themes for a project. If you're like me, you'll find it hard to resist buying lovely fabrics when you come across them in shops, fairs and markets, even when you don't have a particular project in mind. Add these to the bits left over from sewing sessions and you end up with a useful stash of offcuts and remnants. The 25 projects in this book will help you to make the most of this stash. Most of the makes are suitable for medium-weight cotton craft fabrics and, where more substance is required, various interlinings are used to add strength and bulk. Small items and components are made using washable felt.

I hope you find these toys as much fun to make as they were to design. I tested out the toys on my baby granddaughter Violeta and my five-year-old friend Scarlet, and am pleased to report that all the projects met with their approval.

Susie

THE BASICS

MATERIALS & EQUIPMENT

If you are keen on sewing, you will no doubt have most of the tools and equipment needed to complete the projects in this book. All you will have to buy are some fat quarters of fabrics in your choice of colours and designs, plus some felt and trimmings.

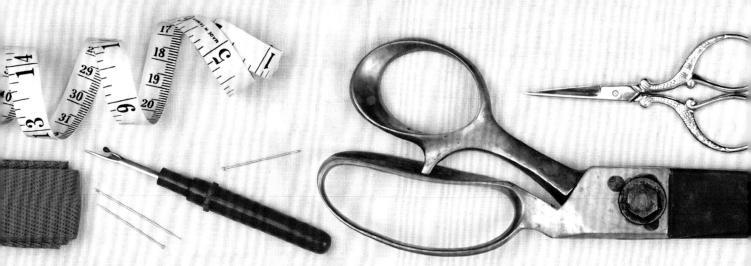

MEASURING You will need a tape measure and a long ruler for drawing lines on fabric. A set square, right-angled ruler or quilter's square helps to measure and mark out neat corners. Use either metric or imperial measurements: both are included in the pattern instructions but do not mix the two.

SCISSORS You will need dress-making scissors for cutting fabrics and small, pointed embroidery scissors for snipping threads. Pinking shears are useful for trimming raw edges on seams, and the ends of ribbons, to prevent fraying; they are also useful for cutting decorative shapes from felt. Use a separate pair of scissors for cutting paper, as paper tends to blunt the blades.

SEAM RIPPER This tool is useful for cutting individual stitches and unpicking seams without damaging the fabric. Insert the pointed blade underneath the stitch to be cut, then push it forward against the thread.

PINS Pinning and basting layers of fabric together prevent them from slipping when stitching by hand or machine. Pins with glass heads are easy to handle and to find. Sometimes, pins distort the fabric or are difficult to use when there are lots of layers or tough fabrics, in which case you may find it easier to use binding clips. Safety pins can be used in place of straight pins to hold fabric layers together; they are also useful for threading elastic and cords through casings.

NEEDLES Sharps are an all-rounder for hand sewing, with a round eye that is easy to thread. For embroidery, an embroidery (crewel) needle has a longer eye, to accommodate thicker thread.

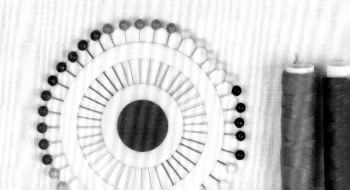

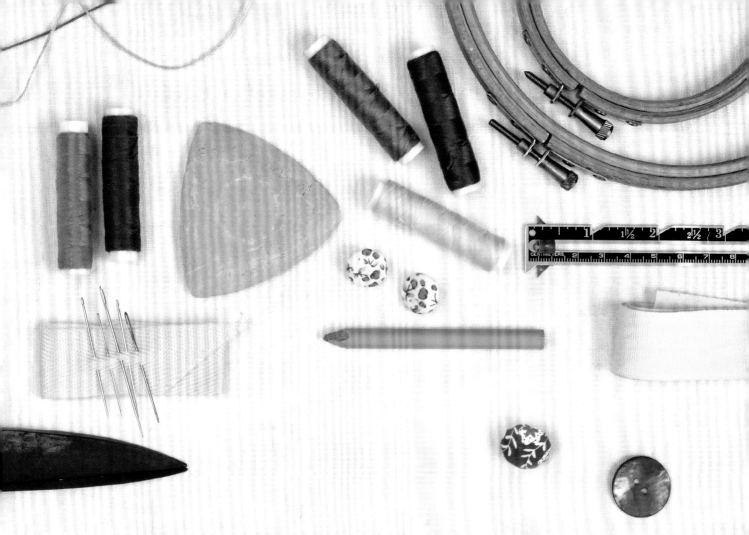

THREADS Use cotton thread when sewing cotton fabrics. It is available in a wide range of colours. Choose a thread to match the fabric as closely as possible, choosing a shade darker if you cannot find an exact match. For decorative stitching, embroidery thread is more substantial than ordinary sewing thread. In most cases, you should place the fabric to be embroidered in an embroidery hoop, to hold it taut while you sew.

BOBBINS Keep a small stock of sewing-machine bobbins loaded with different coloured threads, ready for use. When combining different coloured fabrics, it can be useful to use one colour as a top thread and another on the bobbin.

IRON A good steam iron is an essential piece of equipment, and your ironing board should be firm and stable, with a well-padded surface. Press your fabrics before measuring and cutting, then press the work regularly when sewing, for a neat finish.

FABRICS Cotton fabrics are widely available as pre-cut fat quarters. These have been used throughout the book as the main fabrics for the various toys. Other materials used include velvet and silk. Where felt is used, make sure this is washable. Craft felt will fall apart when it is washed, so buy felt made from wool or a wool blend, and ask when buying if it is suitable for making washable toys. If you are unsure, wash a sample in the washing machine before using it in a project.

TECHNIQUES

The majority of the projects in this book involve basic sewing techniques, both by hand and machine. In this section you will find some basic instructions and tips to help you make your toys as neat and professional-looking as possible, as well as safe and child-friendly.

PREPARING TO SEW

MARKING FABRIC

When a project is made up of squares, rectangles and strips of fabric, measurements are given within the pattern instructions and you will need to measure and mark these out on your fabric. Use a ruler for straight lines, and mark out shapes using tailor's chalk or a dressmaker's chalk pencil, which produce lines that can be rubbed out afterwards. Use a colour that shows up on the fabric. You can also use a water-erasable marker pen. An ordinary pencil can be used where the marks will be hidden in the seams or on the inside of the finished item. Complex pattern pieces are printed as templates at the back of the book. Most will need enlarging on a photocopier.

INTERFACING, LININGS AND STABILIZERS

To add substance and sometimes stiffness to cotton fabrics, other materials are applied to the fabric pieces before they are assembled. The type and weight you need will be specified in the project. Fusible interfacing is a non-woven material that stiffens the fabric; it is available in three weights: light, medium and heavy. Fusible fleece is a soft, felted fabric that adds a little thickness and softness. Wadding and batting – the types used for making quilts – also create extra padding. When using fusible materials, first identify which side of the material is adhesive and place this side face down on the wrong side of the fabric. Place a piece of non-stick baking paper on top, to protect the base plate of the iron. You may also wish to place some scrap fabric between the fabric and the surface of the ironing board. Press with the iron set to medium heat: the heat will melt the adhesive and bond the interfacing or other material to the fabric. Try not to glide the iron as this may cause the layers of fabric and interfacing to shift.

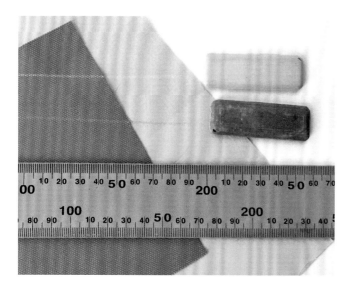

HAND SEWING

BASTING (TACKING)

Basting is used to join layers of fabric together prior to sewing. Use a long running stitch for basting. Start and finish with a couple of stitches worked over each other to secure the end of the thread, and work the stitches within the seam allowance. Running stitch is also used when you want to gather the stitches, for example, when making the carrot on page 120.

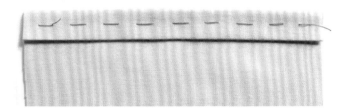

SLIPSTITCH

When making stuffed shapes, you will need to leave a gap that has to be closed after stuffing. Use slipstitch for this. Fold in the raw edges on each side of the gap, then secure the thread in the end of the seam. Use the tip of the needle to pick up a small section of fabric along the fold on one side. Then pick up a small amount of fabric on the other side. Pull the thread to close the gap. Repeat all along the opening and fasten off.

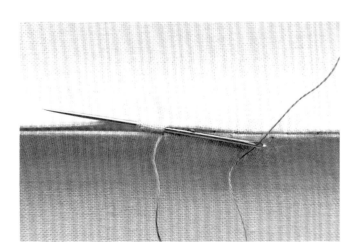

OVERSEWING

This is also known as whipstitch. Place two folded edges of fabric together. Bring the needle through the edge of the back piece and then through the front piece, picking up a small amount of fabric with the needle tip each time. Repeat this process, working from right to left, to join the edges together.

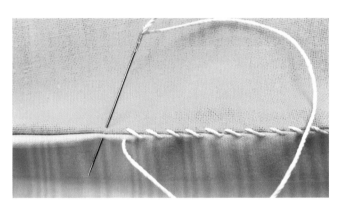

EMBROIDERY

BLANKET STITCH

In this book, blanket stitch is used to attach felt shapes to fabric. Push the needle up through the fabric at the edge of the felt shape and push it back in directly below, through the felt and the fabric. This creates a small loop at the top. Take the needle up through the loop and pull to tighten the stitch; the vertical thread is now held in place by a small horizontal bar that runs along the edge of the felt shape. You can choose the height of the stitch as you insert the needle; you can also alter the space between stitches.

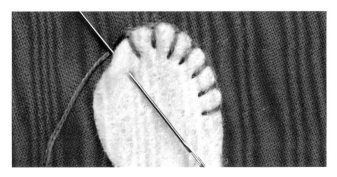

BACKSTITCH

Bring the needle up through the fabric at the start of the line to be stitched. Take the needle back through the fabric one stitch length to the left. Then push the needle back up through the fabric another stitch length to the left, back into the fabric at the end of the first stitch, then back up once again a stitch length to the left. On the wrong side of the fabric, the stitches overlap, making this a strong stitch for sewing hand-stitched seams.

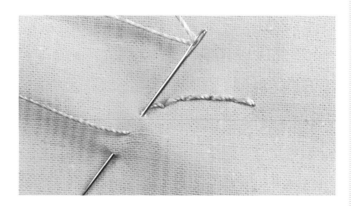

DETACHED CHAIN

Bring the needle up through the fabric and down again at the same point, then up again, a stitch length above the first point and looping the thread around the tip of the needle. Pull through to form a chain loop, then take the needle over the loop of the thread and down through the fabric to secure the stitch with a tiny bar.

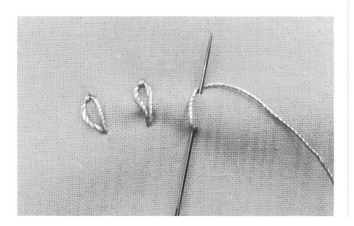

SPLIT STITCH

This stitch is useful for outlining, embroidering lines and filling larger shapes.

1 Thread the needle with the desired number of strands of embroidery thread. Bring the needle up through the fabric at the beginning of the line or outline, then down a little way along. Bring the needle up through the centre of the stitch you just made. Take the needle back down through the fabric a little way along; keep the stitches reasonably short – about $1/8$–$3/16$in (3–5mm in length). Repeat the process along the length of the line.

2 For thicker lines, or to fill shapes, work a second or further rows of split stitches parallel to the first.

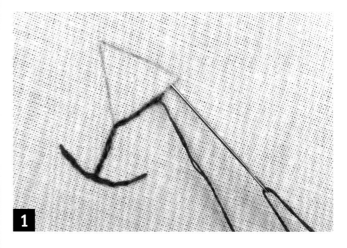

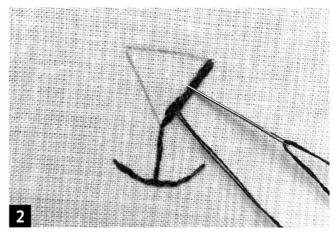

SATIN STITCH

This is suitable for filling very small shapes. The stitches should be short, so they will not be snagged by tiny fingers. Work straight, parallel stitches closely together to cover the shape to be filled. There should be no gaps between stitches. Try to keep the edges smooth and taut to ensure all your stitches lie flat.

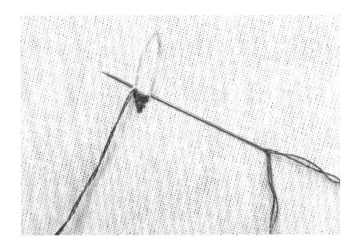

MACHINE SEWING

Most of the toys are made using a sewing machine to ensure that components are firmly joined together. Straight stitch is used for seams while zigzag stitch is used to outline appliqué shapes. Use the right size needle for the fabric – size 80 for medium-weight cotton – and change it frequently to ensure that the needle is sharp.

SETTING UP

Place the sewing machine where there is plenty of light and you can sit comfortably. Make sure that the machine is threaded correctly and that the threads from the needle and the bobbin are placed away from you, towards the back of the base plate. When you start to stitch, turn the hand wheel to lower the needle into the fabric; this will help to prevent the threads from tangling. Before stitching your project, test the machine-stitch size and tension on a scrap of the fabric you are working with, and adjust if necessary.

STRAIGHT STITCH

This is used for flat seams and topstitching, and for hemming. You can alter the length of the stitch, using a long stitch for basting and gathering, for example. At the start and end of a line of stitching, backstitch for a few stitches. This will prevent the stitches from coming undone and you can snip off the threads close to the surface of the fabric.

TOPSTITCHING

Topstitching creates a crisp finish and holds layers of fabric neatly and securely in place. Press the seam to one side. Topstitch parallel to the seamline; the distance from the line is variable, but on a seam it will be a smaller measurement than the seam allowance, to ensure that the raw edges of the fabric are trapped under the topstitching.

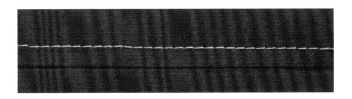

ZIGZAG STITCH

For appliqué shapes, a close zigzag stitch is used all around the edges to attach the shape to the fabric and prevent raw edges from fraying.

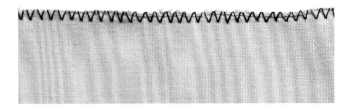

ADDITIONAL TECHNIQUES

BINDING EDGES

When binding an uneven edge, a corner or curve, two-step binding is the preferred method.

1 Open out the binding and line up one raw edge of the binding with the edge of the fabric. Pin and baste to hold in place, then stitch along the foldline by hand or machine.

2 Fold the binding over to enclose the raw edges, and slipstitch the other long folded edge of the binding on the seamline.

ONE-STEP BINDING

One-step binding works best on a straight edge of firm fabric. Fold the binding in half down its length and press. Place the folded binding over the edge of the fabric, to enclose it completely. Pin and baste in place, then machine stitch close to the lower edge of the binding, checking on the other side of the work that the stitching has captured both long edges of the binding.

CLIPPING CURVES AND CORNERS

On curved seams, cut 'V' shapes into the seam allowance, close to the stitchline. Snip very carefully with small, sharp scissors to avoid cutting through the stitches by mistake. Corners should be cut across at an angle so they are sharp when the work is turned right sides out.

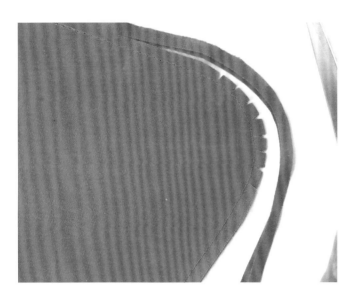

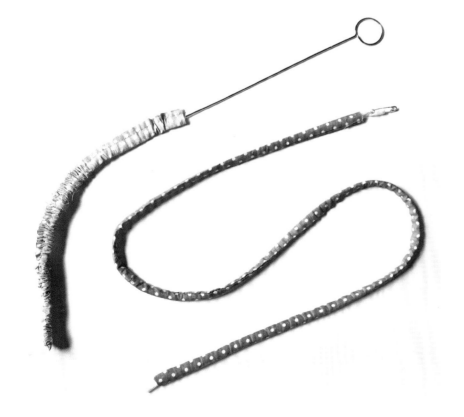

LOOP TURNER

Making a narrow tube of fabric can be fiddly, but the task is easier if you use a loop turner: this is a long metal pin with a ring on one end and a clip on the other. Cut a strip of fabric to the length required and twice the width of the finished tube, then add ¾in (2cm) for the seam. Fold in half lengthways, right sides together, aligning the long edges, and stitch a ⅜in (1cm) seam. Trim the seam allowance to ³⁄₁₆in (5mm). Insert the loop turner into the tube of fabric and attach the clip to the end of the seam, then pull the loop turner back through the tube.

BABY'S
FIRST TOYS

SEGMENTED BALL

This bright and colourful ball is soft and squidgy – the perfect texture for little hands to hold and explore. It is suitable for indoor play and has a bell inside that makes a pleasing sound. Throw it, roll it, squeeze it; even the tiniest baby will find this ball delightful.

Find the template on page 134

You will need
Scraps of fabric, measuring at least 12 x 5in (30 x 12.75cm), in each of six plain colours
Toy stuffing
Bell
Film canister or small lidded plastic box
Dressmaker's chalk pencil or fabric marker
Card for making template
Pins
Dress-making scissors
General-purpose scissors
Sewing machine
Sewing needle
Thread to match fabrics
Iron and ironing board

NOTE: The seam allowance is $3/8$in (1cm).

Finished size is roughly:
21in (54cm) in circumference

1 Place the fabrics in a neat stack; press them first if necessary. Make a card template using the pattern piece and mark the segment shape on the top piece of fabric. Pin all layers together and cut out.

2 Place two of the fabric pieces with right sides together and pin along one curved edge.

3 Stitch along the curved edge with a ⅜in (1cm) seam. Start and end the seam ⅜in (1cm) from the edge and make sure you backstitch at the beginning and end of the seam so that it doesn't come undone.

4 Join a third segment to the second curved edge of one of the pieces.

5 Repeat steps 2–4 with the remaining three pieces of fabric. You now have two halves of the ball.

6 Join the two halves of the ball by lining up the edges and machine stitching together, making sure you leave a gap of approximately 4in (10cm) in the centre of one of the seams. Trim both ends.

7 Turn right side out through the gap in the seam. Stuff firmly with toy filling. Place the bell inside the film canister, close the lid, then position it in the centre of the stuffing.

8 Turn the seam allowance to the inside on the opening, then slipstitch the folded edges securely together to close the gap (see page 15).

Tip

Place the bell inside a small container with a lid, such as a film canister or plastic box, so that the bell doesn't work its way through the stuffing. For extra security, you may wish to glue the lid in place.

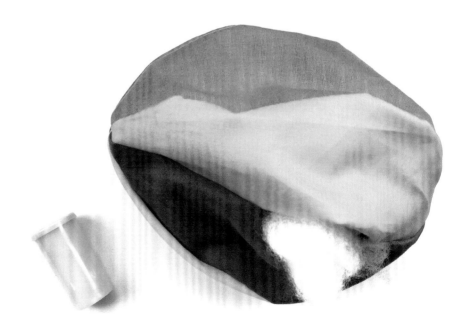

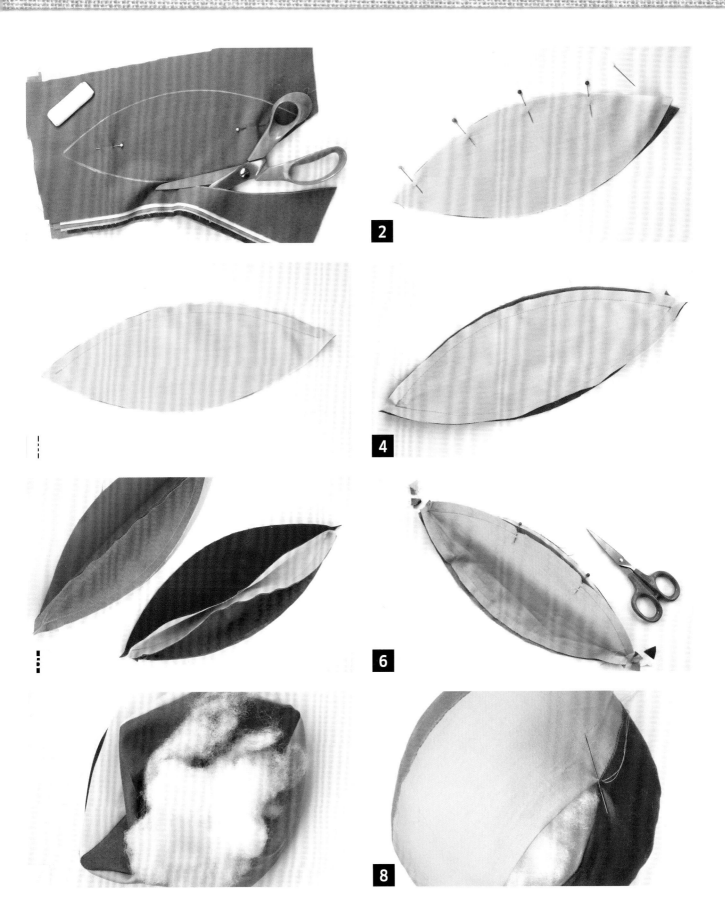

TIGER-CUB RATTLE

This stripy tiger-cub rattle will stimulate your baby's senses. Small enough for tiny hands to clutch, it has a soft, pleasing texture, with a design created by hand embroidery. The rattle inside makes it fun to shake.

Find the template on page 132

You will need
1 fat quarter of plain cream fabric
7 x 6in (18 x 15cm) polyester wadding
Six-stranded embroidery thread in orange,
    pink and black
Polyester toy filling
Small rattle or squeaker
Erasable fabric marker
Embroidery hoop
Pins
Dress-making scissors
General-purpose scissors
Corner and edge shaper or similar tool, such as a knitting needle
Sewing machine
Sewing needle
Embroidery (crewel) needle
Thread to match fabric
Thread for basting
Iron and ironing board

NOTE: There are many sound-making devices available to buy. This toy is quite small, so choose a rattle or squeaker with a flattish shape to fit inside.

Finished size is roughly:
6 x 5in (15 x 12.75cm)

1 Use the template to trace the shapes on to the fabric, using an erasable fabric marker.

2 Place the fabric in an embroidery hoop. Thread an embroidery needle with two strands of orange embroidery thread and embroider the tiger's stripes in satin stitch (see page 17).

3 With two strands of pink thread, fill the nose shape with satin stitch. Use black thread to embroider the eyes in satin stitch and the mouth in split stitch (see page 16). Embroider the stripes on the other piece.

4 Cut out the tiger shapes. Cut the same shapes from polyester wadding and place wadding on wrong side of each embroidered shape. Pin and baste all round, within the seam allowance.

5 Place the two tiger pieces, right sides together. Pin, baste and stitch with a $5/16$in (8mm) seam, leaving a $1\frac{1}{2}$in (4cm) gap along the back leg, for turning. Clip corners and snip into the seam allowance on the curves (see page 19).

6 Turn right side out with the help of a corner and edge shaper or similar tool, such as a knitting needle. Stuff firmly, but do not overstuff. Insert the rattle or squeaker so that it sits in the centre of the body.

7 Turn the raw edges to the inside and pin folded edges together. Slipstitch to close the gap (see page 15).

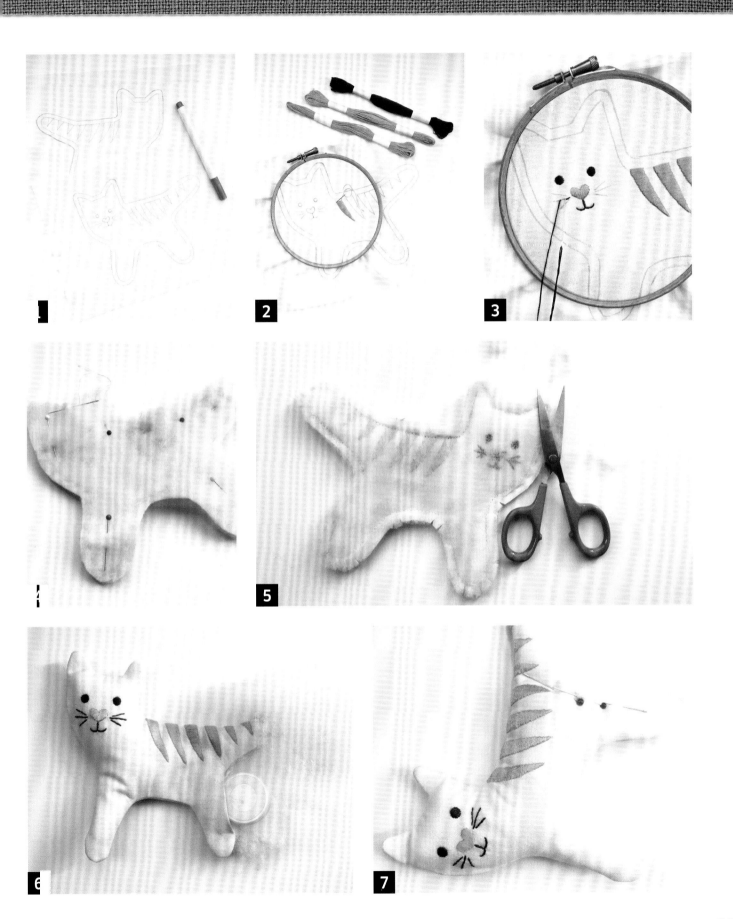

OCTOPUS

This sea creature with a friendly face is soft, round and squishy, making it perfect for cuddling. The bright, rainbow-coloured tentacles will attract a young baby's attention and they are just the right shape and size for little hands to grasp.

Find the templates on pages 132–33

You will need
1 fat quarter of spot-printed fabric
Scraps of plain fabrics in pink, coral, turquoise, blue, lilac, orange, green and yellow
Small scraps of felt in white, pale blue and pink
Six-stranded embroidery thread to match or contrast with felt colours
Polyester toy filling
Dressmaker's chalk pencil or fabric marker
Card for making template
Pins
Dress-making scissors
General-purpose scissors
Sewing machine
Sewing needle
Embroidery (crewel) needle
Thread for basting
Thread to match fabric
Iron and ironing board

NOTE: You can choose your own palette of plain colours: the brighter, the better.

Finished size is roughly:
Body: 5¾in (14.5cm) high with a circumference of 19in (48cm)
Each tentacle: 6½in (16cm) long

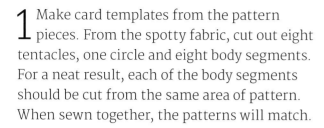

1 Make card templates from the pattern pieces. From the spotty fabric, cut out eight tentacles, one circle and eight body segments. For a neat result, each of the body segments should be cut from the same area of pattern. When sewn together, the patterns will match.

2 Cut out one tentacle from each of eight plain colours. Draw around the card template with a chalk pencil, using a colour that shows up clearly to make cutting easier.

3 Place two of the spotty fabric body pieces with right sides together. Pin, then stitch along one curved edge with a $5/16$in (8mm) seam, starting and ending the seam $5/16$in (8mm) from the point at the top. Add a third segment to the first two, then a fourth.

4 Join the remaining four body segments in the same way, then join the two halves by lining up the edges and machine stitching together.

5 Press the edges of the seams open.

6 Cut out two circles 1in (2.5cm) in diameter from white felt and two smaller circles, $5/8$in (1.5cm) in diameter from pale blue. Cut out a curved mouth from pink felt. Pin in place, using the photo of the finished octopus as a guide.

7 Thread an embroidery needle with two strands of embroidery thread in colours to match or contrast with the felt, and stitch around the eyes and mouth with blanket stitch (see page 15). (Note that this photo shows the octopus stuffed.)

8 Make the tentacles. For each one, match a spotty fabric piece with a coloured piece and stitch all around the curved edge with a $5/16$in (8mm) seam allowance. Leave short edges open for turning. Snip into the seam allowance on the top curve (see page 19).

9 Turn each tentacle right side out and stuff. Do not add too much filling, and leave about 1in (2.5cm) empty at the top. Pin the tentacles to the body, lining up each body seam with the centre of one of the tentacles. Baste the tentacles in place, within the $5/16$in (8mm) seam allowance.

10 Turn the body wrong side out. Tuck all the tentacles inside the body. Place the spotted-fabric circle on top, to form the base, and pin all around. Baste, then stitch with a $5/16$in (8mm) seam, leaving a gap of about 2in (5cm) for turning.

11 Snip into the seam allowance all around, then turn right side out. Stuff the octopus body firmly. Turn the raw edges of the gap to the inside. Pin and slipstitch folded edges together securely (see page 15).

Tip

You could put a bell, rattle or squeaker inside the octopus so that it makes a noise when it's being played with.

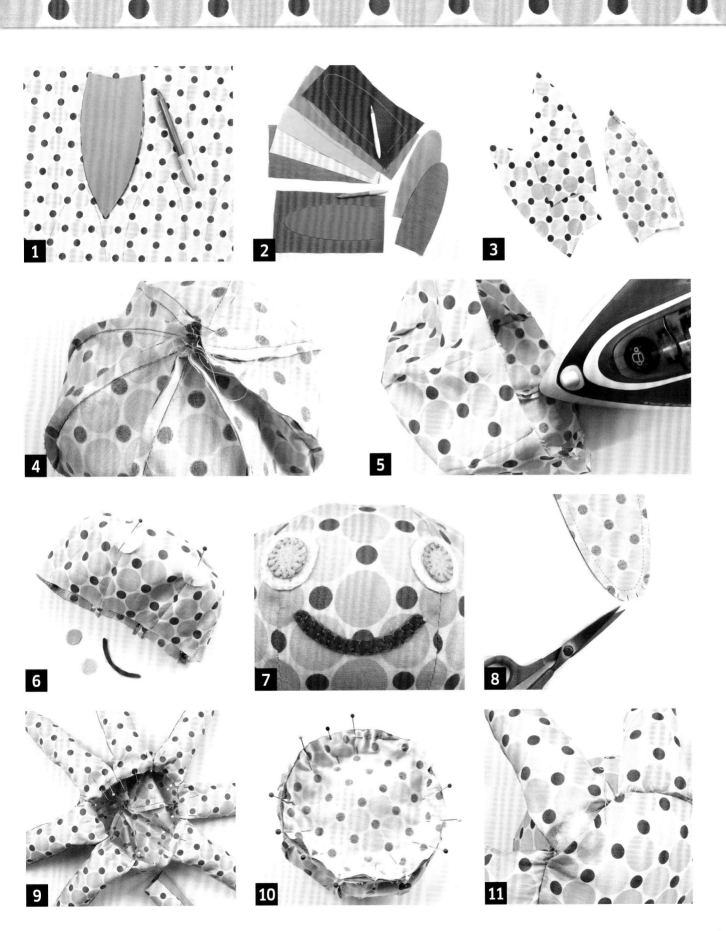

RABBIT CUDDLE BLANKET

Lots of babies rely on a comfort blanket to soothe and settle them — so here is a soft little blanket with a friendly rabbit face for cuddly companionship. Perfect for snuggling up with, this easy-to-wash blanket is sure to be loved for several years.

Find the templates on page 134

You will need
1 fat quarter of printed cotton fabric
1 fat quarter of plain cotton fabric
1 fat quarter of dimple fleece fabric
Small scraps of felt in pink and black
Erasable fabric marker
Embroidery hoop
Six-stranded embroidery thread in pink, grey and black
Pins
Dress-making scissors
General-purpose scissors
Quilter's square or ruler
Corner and edge shaper or similar tool, such as a knitting needle
Sewing machine
Sewing needle
Embroidery (crewel) needle
Thread to match fabric
Thread for basting
Iron and ironing board

Finished size is roughly:
17in (43cm) square

1 From both the patterned cotton and the fleece, cut a 17½in (44.5cm) square. From the fleece and the plain cotton, use the templates to cut out two ear shapes. Mark out the head shapes on the plain cotton. On one of these, mark out the features using an erasable fabric marker; do not cut this out yet.

2 Place the face piece in an embroidery hoop. Cut nose and eye shapes from the scraps of felt and pin in place.

3 Thread an embroidery needle with two strands of pink embroidery thread and embroider all around the edge of the nose with blanket stitch (see page 15), keeping the stitches small and close together. With two strands of black thread, outline the eyes in blanket stitch, then embroider the mouth in split stitch (see page 16).

4 Remove the head shape from the hoop and press. Place pairs of shapes together: the head and the two ears. Pin, baste and stitch with a 5/16in (8mm) seam, leaving the lower straight edge of each ear and the two straight edges on the head open. Snip into the seam allowance on all curved edges (see page 19).

5 Turn the ears and head right sides out and press lightly. Pin the head piece to one corner of the patterned cotton square, matching edges. Place the ears, fleece side up, to the centre of each of the straight edges of the head. Baste.

6 Place the fleece square, wrong side up, on the fabric square, covering the head and ears. Pin all around edges. Baste, then stitch, leaving a gap of approximately 4in (10cm) in the centre of one side.

7 Clip the corners and turn right side out. Use a corner and edge shaper, or a knitting needle or similar object, to push out each corner for a neat result.

8 Turn the raw edges of the gap to the inside and pin the folded edges together, then slipstitch securely (see page 15).

Tip

Dimple fleece has a soft, short pile with little raised spots all over. It is also excellent for making baby quilts and dressing gowns.

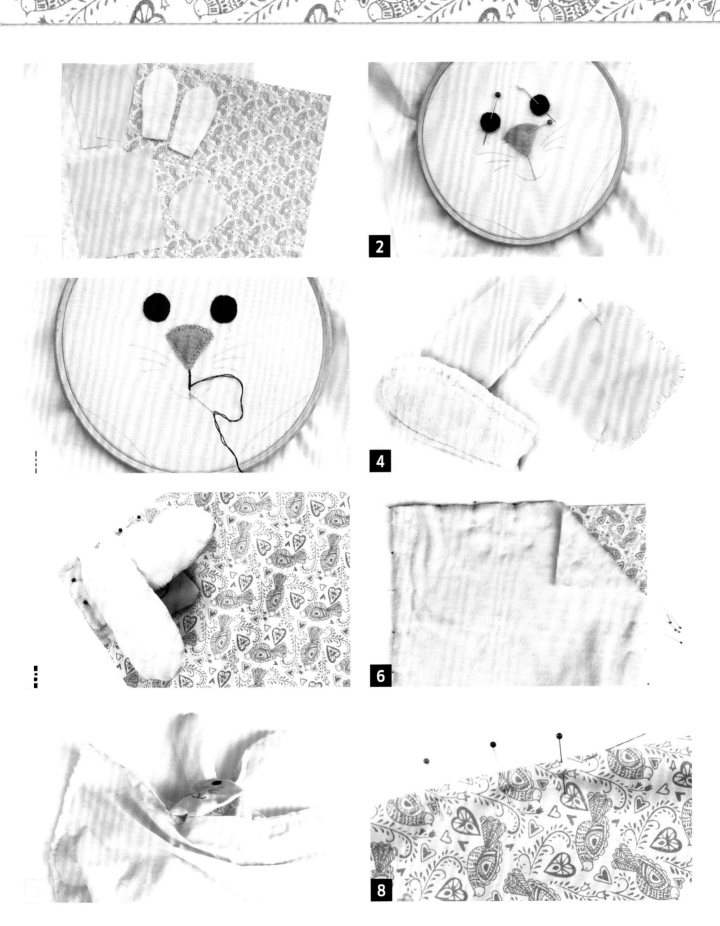

ANIMAL FRIENDS

MOUSE

Small enough to slip into a pocket, this simple, cute mouse makes a great companion to carry around. It is guaranteed to appeal to children of all ages. You could make several mice and use them for storytelling and for teaching nursery rhymes.

Find the templates on page 135

You will need
Scraps of patterned and plain-coloured fabrics
Six-stranded black embroidery thread
Polyester toy filling
Dressmaker's chalk pencil or fabric marker
Card for making template
Pins
Dress-making scissors
General-purpose scissors
Loop turner (see page 19)
Corner and edge shaper or similar tool, such as a knitting needle
Sewing machine
Sewing needle
Embroidery (crewel) needle
Thread to match fabric
Iron and ironing board

NOTE: This project is great for making use of small scraps of fabric left over from other projects. You can make the mouse with the same fabric all over – you will need a piece approximately 8in (20cm) square. Alternatively, you can use contrast fabrics for the tail and the ears.

Finished size is roughly:
4¾in (12cm) long, excluding tail

1 Using the templates, cut out one top piece, two ears and two side pieces from patterned fabric. If you are cutting them from a single thickness of fabric, draw one side piece, then flip the template over to draw the other. Cut out two ears from plain fabric.

2 To make the ears, place main fabric piece and plain lining right sides together and stitch all around curved edge with a ¼in (6mm) seam. Leave the straight bottom edge open. Snip into seam allowance on curves (see page 19).

3 Turn the ears right side out. Press. Make a small pleat in the centre of the lower edges. Pin and stitch to the top piece, one on each side, between the marks.

4 To make a tail, cut a strip of matching or contrasting fabric 6 x 1¼in (15 x 3cm). Fold it in half lengthways and stitch ¼in (6mm) from raw edges along the length and across one short end. Leave the other end open for turning.

5 Turn right side out using a loop turner (see page 19). Press.

6 Pin the tail to the end of the top piece. Make sure it is clear of the sides so that it doesn't get trapped in the seams.

7 Pin one side section to the top piece, then stitch with a ⁵⁄₁₆in (8mm) seam, beginning and ending ⁵⁄₁₆in (8mm) from each end.

8 Pin and stitch the other side to the top piece, then stitch the two side pieces together along the base (straight edge), leaving a gap of 2in (5cm) in the centre of the seam, for turning.

9 Turn the mouse right side out, and stuff firmly. Push the filling right into the point of the snout using a corner and edge shaper or similar tool, such as a knitting needle.

10 Turn the raw edges of the gap to the inside and slipstitch the folded edges together securely (see page 15).

11 Thread an embroidery needle with two strands of black thread and embroider the nose in satin stitch. Mark the position of the eyes on each side and embroider each one in satin stitch (see page 17), taking the needle through the head to the other side as you do so. When you have finished embroidering, pull the needle back into the body of the mouse. Pull it taut, then cut the thread close to the body to lose the end of the thread inside the mouse.

Tip

If you are making several mice, make card templates of the pattern pieces. Place these templates on the fabric and draw around them. This makes cutting out multiple fabric pieces quick and easy.

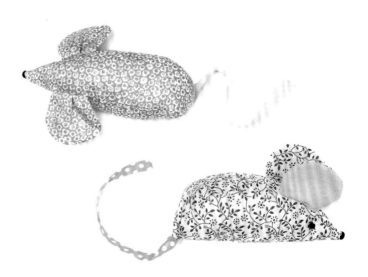

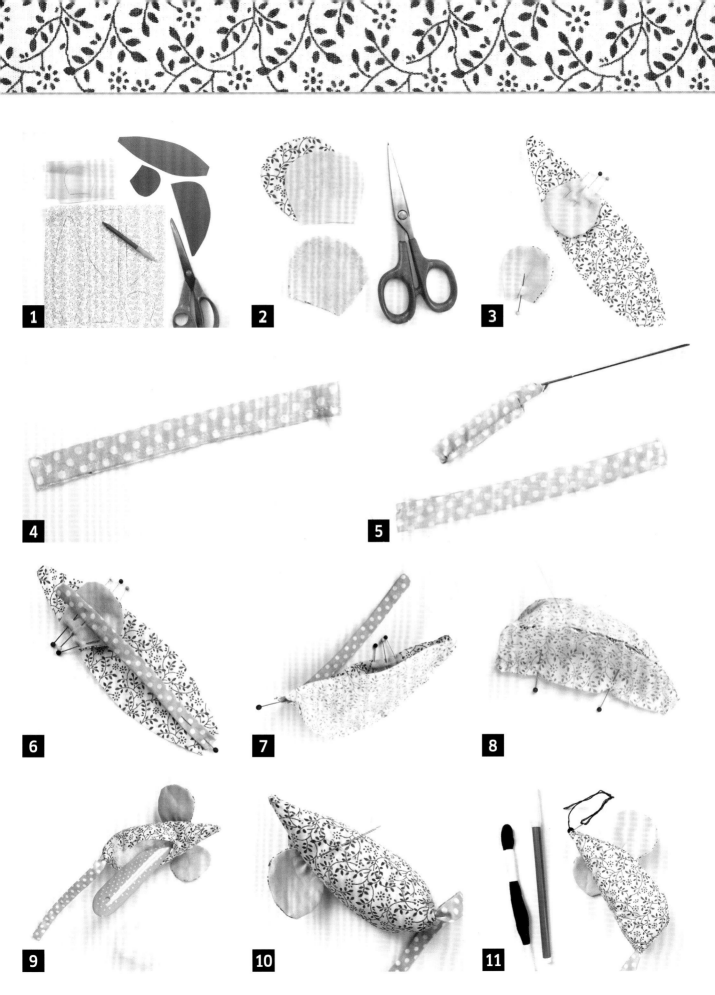

OWL

Owls are popular with children of all ages, as well as adults. This one has soft wings and feet, and a little pocket to explore. The embroidered eyes make this owl suitable for a baby, but it might find older fans, too!

Find the templates on page 135

You will need
1 fat quarter of main fabric
8in (20cm) square of each of two contrasting patterned fabrics
5in (12.75cm) square of plain fabric
Scraps of felt in pale yellow, yellow and brown
Six-stranded embroidery thread in matching or contrasting colour
Polyester toy filling
Dressmaker's chalk pencil or fabric marker
Card for making template
Pins
Dress-making scissors
General-purpose scissors
Corner and edge shaper or similar tool, such as a knitting needle
Sewing machine
Sewing needle
Embroidery (crewel) needle
Thread for basting
Thread to match fabric
Iron and ironing board

Finished size is roughly:
8in (20cm) high and 5½in (14cm) wide

1 Make card templates from the pattern pieces. From main fabric, mark out and cut one owl body and head shape, four wing shapes and one 6¼in (15.75cm) square. From one of the contrast fabrics, cut out four wing shapes and a rectangle measuring 6¼ x 4¾in (15.75 x 12cm), for the head. From the other contrast fabric, cut out four wing shapes and one rectangle measuring 5½ x 4⅛in (14 x 10.5cm), for the pocket. From plain fabric, cut out four feet shapes.

2 With right sides facing, join the square and the 6¼ x 4¾in (15.75 x 12cm) rectangle with a ⅜in (1cm) seam. Press the seam to one side. Place the body and head template on the fabric with the line level with the seam. Draw around and cut out the shape.

3 For the eyes, cut two circles from pale yellow felt and two circles from brown felt, using the templates. Cut a beak shape from yellow felt using the template.

4 Thread an embroidery needle with two strands of embroidery thread and sew the features in place using blanket stitch (see page 15).

5 To make the pocket, fold the rectangle of fabric in half lengthways with right sides together, and stitch the sides with a ¼in (6mm) seam. Turn right side out and press. Pin and stitch to the owl front, placing the raw edges of the pocket centrally on the lower edge of the owl.

6 Make the feet. Place two pieces right sides together and stitch all around with a ¼in (6mm) seam, leaving the straight edge open. Snip into the seam allowance on curves, and turn right side out, using a corner and edge shaper or similar tool, such as a knitting needle, to push out the shape.

7 Pin the feet in place, as shown, lining up the side edge of each one with the sides of the pocket.

8 Stitch together pairs of wing pieces, right sides facing, leaving the straight edges open for turning. Snip into the seam allowance on curves and turn each one right side out. Use a corner and edge shaper or similar tool to push out the shape.

9 Pin three wing pieces on each side of the owl, as shown. Baste in place.

10 Place the back piece on top, face down, aligning all edges. Stitch with a ⁵⁄₁₆in (8mm) seam, leaving an opening of 2in (5cm) on one side for turning.

11 Turn right side out and stuff lightly – do not overstuff. Turn raw edges on opening to inside and slipstitch closed (see page 15).

TORTOISE

If you like patchwork, you will love this little fellow. Six-sided patches of fabric fit together to form a domed shell, from which the tortoise's head, tail and feet peep out. Toddlers will also appreciate the tortoise for imaginative play.

Find the templates on page 136

You will need
1 fat quarter of printed fabric
1 fat quarter of plain blue fabric
Various scraps of plain and printed fabrics
8in (20cm) square of fusible fleece
Six-stranded dark brown embroidery thread
Polyester toy filling
Dressmaker's chalk pencil or fabric marker
Thin card for making templates
Pins
Dress-making scissors
General-purpose scissors
Corner and edge shaper or similar tool, such as a knitting needle
Tweezers
Sewing machine
Sewing needle
Embroidery (crewel) needle
Thread to match fabric
Thread for basting
Iron and ironing board

Finished size is roughly:
7½ x 7½in (19 x 19cm)

NOTE: The patches are joined using the English pieced method, which involves wrapping fabric around thin card to make crisply formed shapes that are sewn together by hand. Once sewn, the papers are removed.

1 Using the smaller shape templates, cut one hexagon from card for the centre of the top shell, six of the other six-sided shapes and six triangles. Using the larger template, cut fabric patches: one hexagon and six half-hexagons from the main fabric and three pairs of the other six-sided shapes from the other patterned fabrics. From plain fabric, using the head, leg and tail templates, cut two heads, two tails and eight legs. From main fabric, using the base template, cut a circle for the base.

2 Pair the head, tail and leg pieces and stitch together with a ¼in (6mm) seam, leaving the bottom straight edge of each one open.

3 Snip into the seam allowance on each one (see page 19). Turn right side out using a corner and edge shaper or similar tool. Use tweezers to push the stuffing into the corners, then put these pieces to one side.

4 Place a card shape centrally on each of the fabric patches. On each one, fold the fabric over the edge of the card and stitch through all layers – card and fabric – around all six sides. The half-hexagons will now be triangle shapes.

5 Place one six-sided shape alongside the central hexagon, matching the edges, and oversew together (see page 15). The needle should pick up a small piece of the fabric from each folded edge. Be careful not to sew through the card at the same time.

6 Add a second patch in the same way, and keep adding patches until they are all attached along their top edge to the central hexagon.

7 Remove the basting stitches from the centre patch, then remove the card. Now join each six-sided shape patch to its neighbour along their long edges, as shown.

8 Join the triangles to the lower edges of the six-sided shapes to fill in the gaps and complete the upper shell. Remove the basting stitches and the pieces of card. Press the edges with a hot iron.

9 Pin the head, tail and legs to the patchwork shell, positioning each one centrally on one of the six-sided patches. Baste in place.

10 Use the base template to cut a circle of fusible fleece and apply to the wrong side of the fabric circle with a hot iron. With the fabric side facing down, place the circle on top of the upper shell and pin all around. Baste, then stitch with a 5/16in (8mm) seam, leaving a gap of approximately 2½in (6.5cm) for turning.

11 Snip into the seam allowance all around (see page 19), then turn right side out and stuff. Turn under the raw edges on the opening and pin together, then slipstitch to close the gap (see page 15).

12 Thread an embroidery needle with two strands of embroidery thread and embroider an eye in satin stitch on each side of the head (see page 17).

Tip

When you join the patches, make sure your oversewing stitches are small, closely spaced and firm to achieve a neat result.

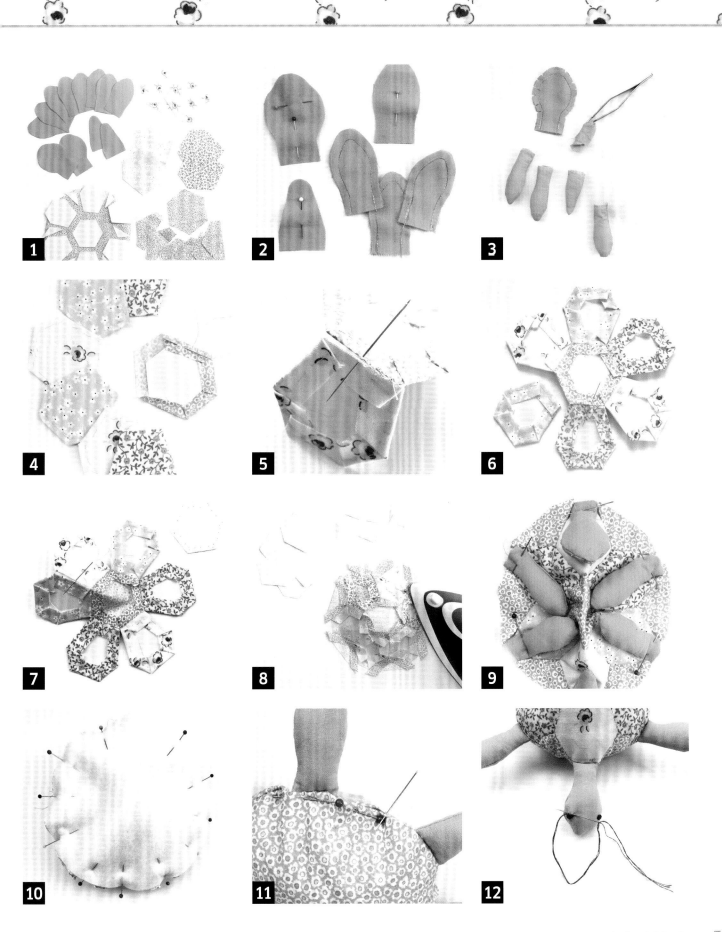

TEDDY BEAR

A little teddy is a universal favourite. This one, made from a combination of pretty print fabrics, has a simple flat shape. It's relatively easy to make and great to cuddle. Softly stuffed, with a hidden squeaker, it is suitable for a baby.

Find the templates on page 137

You will need
4 contrasting printed cotton fabrics: 2 pieces 12 x 6in
  (30 x 15cm) and 2 pieces 12 x 4in (30 x 10cm)
2¼ x 2in (6 x 5cm) pale peach felt
12in (30cm) square of fusible fleece
Small squeaker
Toy stuffing
Erasable fabric marker
Embroidery hoop
Six-stranded embroidery thread in pale peach
  and dark grey
Pins
Dress-making scissors
General-purpose scissors
Sewing machine
Sewing needle
Embroidery (crewel) needle
Thread to match fabric
Dark grey thread
Thread for basting
Iron and ironing board

Finished size is roughly:
11½in (29cm) tall

NOTE: You can use fabrics left over from other projects to make this teddy. The largest pieces should be at least 12 x 6in (30 x 15cm) in order to cut out the main body shape.

1 From each of two contrasting fabrics, cut two rectangles measuring 12 x 4in (30 x 10cm). Join the contrasting pairs with a $^5/_{16}$in (8mm) seam and press the seams to one side. Topstitch the seams (see page 17).

2 Use the template to draw the head and body shape on the joined pieces, with the seam running along the centre. Cut four arm shapes from a third patterned fabric and four ears from a fourth. Cut a muzzle shape from felt.

3 Place the muzzle on one of the heads and pin it in position. Thread an embroidery needle with two strands of embroidery thread to match the colour of the felt and stitch the muzzle in place with blanket stitch (see page 15). Use the template to mark the features on to the muzzle.

4 Thread an embroidery needle with two strands of dark grey thread and embroider the nose and mouth in split stitch (see page 16), covering the marks you have drawn.

5 Cut out the two head and body shapes. Use the template to cut two pieces from fusible fleece. Apply to the wrong side of the fabric pieces, using a hot iron.

6 Make the arms and ears. Place two matching pieces right sides together and stitch with a $^5/_{16}$in (8mm) seam. Snip into the seam allowance on curves (see page 19) and turn right side out.

7 Stuff the arms and ears lightly, leaving the top $^1/_2$in (1.25cm) of each one unfilled. Pin and baste in place on one of the body pieces.

8 Place the other body piece on top, face down and matching edges. Pin and baste together.

9 Stitch with a $^5/_{16}$in (8mm) seam, leaving a gap of approximately 3in (7.5cm) on one side. Snip into the seam allowance on all curves and turn right side out.

10 Stuff the head and legs first, then add a squeaker, placing it in the tummy area, and stuff the body area.

11 Turn the raw edges of the gap to the inside and slipstitch the edges together to close (see page 15).

Tip

After embroidering the features, you can remove any visible blue marks from the erasable fabric marker using a cotton bud dampened with water.

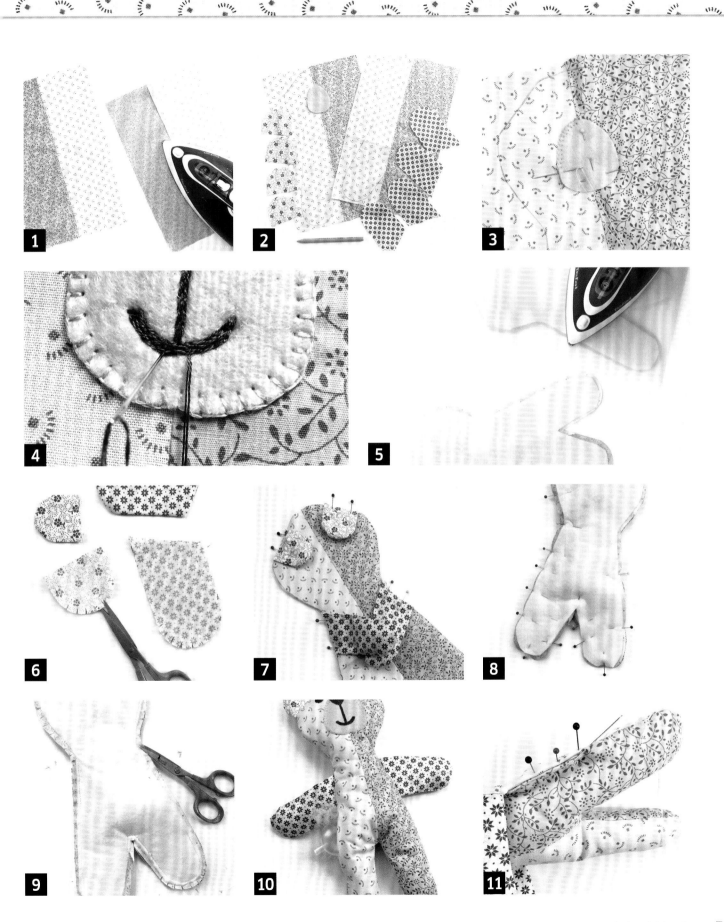

GIRAFFE

Choose an attractive spotty fabric for this cuddly companion, with a smaller spot as the contrast fabric. A baby's hand can easily fit around the giraffe's long narrow neck and legs, and the ears and tail will prove fun to pull.

Find the templates on page 138

You will need
1 fat quarter of cotton fabric with large spot print (main)
1 fat quarter of cotton fabric with smaller spot print (contrast)
Toy stuffing
Pins
Dress-making scissors
General-purpose scissors
Sewing machine
Sewing needle
Thread for basting
Thread to match fabric
Iron and ironing board
Corner and edge turner or similar tool, such as a knitting needle

NOTE: The seam allowance for the main part of the giraffe is ⅜in (1cm) but for the tail and ears it is ¼in (6mm), to avoid bulk on these smaller components.

Finished size is roughly:
14in (35.5cm) high

1 Make a pattern using the templates. Fold the large spot fabric across the width and the smaller spot fabric along the length. Pin the pattern to the fabric and cut out the pieces.

2 You will have two body pieces and two ears cut from the main fabric, and two belly pieces, two ears and two tail pieces from the contrast fabric.

3 Pin and baste the two belly pieces together along the top edge. Stitch with a ⅜in (1cm) seam. Remove the basting thread, clip into the seam allowance on the curves (see page 19), and press the seam open.

4 With right sides together, pin and baste the legs together: main fabric and contrast fabric. The longer pieces at one end of the belly should be pinned to the front of the neck.

5 Stitch seams together. Snip into the seam allowance on corners and curves.

6 Place the two tail pieces right sides together, pin and stitch all around with a ¼in (6mm) seam, leaving the narrow end open. Turn right side out.

7 Pin the body pieces together, sandwiching the tail in the seam allowance at the back end. Mark a gap of about 3½in (9cm) at the front of the neck with pins. Stitch all round with a ⅜in (1cm) seam, leaving a gap between the pins.

8 Turn right side out, using a device such as a knitting needle or a corner and edge turner, to push out corners and curved seams.

9 Stuff firmly, pushing the stuffing into every part using a corner and edge shaper, or knitting needle.

10 Turn the seam allowances to the inside at the opening, then pin the folded edges together and slipstitch securely to close the gap (see page 15).

11 Place the pairs of ear pieces, main and contrast, with right sides together, baste and stitch, leaving the short end open, then turn right side out. Press.

12 Turn the seam allowance to the inside on the opening of each ear, then pin the folded edges together and slipstitch to close the gap. Pin the ears to the head on either side, and hand stitch securely in place.

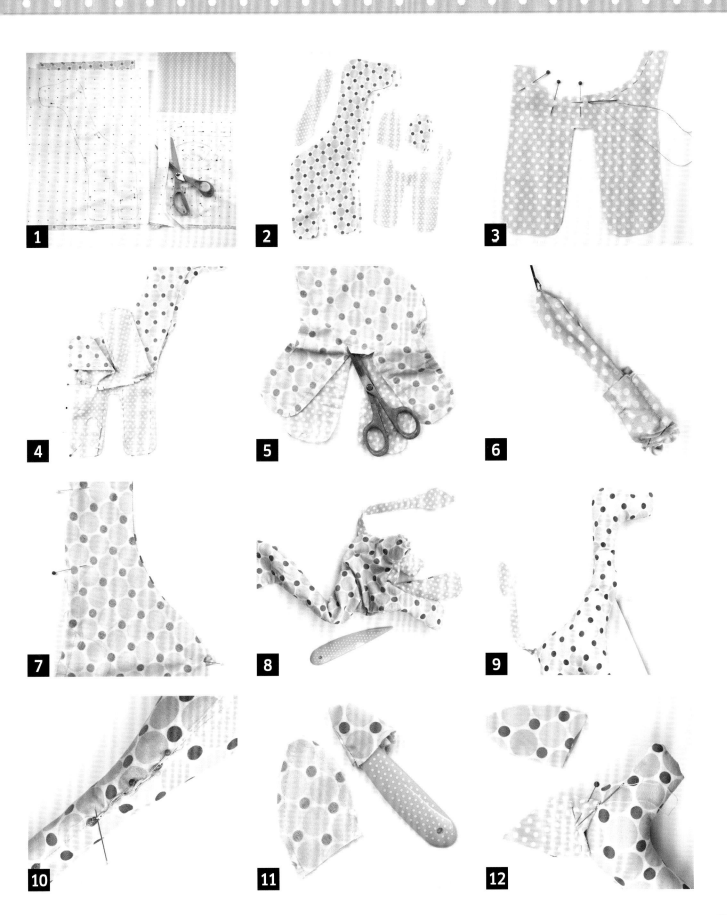

FOX IN SLEEPING BAG

The perfect companion for cuddling during bedtime stories, this sleepy fox has her own cosy patchwork sleeping bag when it's time for bed. Babies will love putting their foxy friend in the bag and getting her out again!

Find the templates for the fox
    on page 139

You will need
1 fat quarter of plain cotton fabric in orange
1 fat quarter of plain cotton fabric in cream
Scraps of printed cotton fabric in five different patterns
20½ x 8¾in (52 x 22cm) of lightweight batting
5½ x 4in (14 x 10cm) of white felt
Small scrap of black felt
Six-stranded embroidery thread in white and black
Toy stuffing
40in (1m) of 1in (2.5cm) bias binding in orange
Dressmaker's chalk pencil or fabric marker
Pins
Dress-making scissors
Sewing machine
Sewing needle
Embroidery (crewel) needle
Thread to match fabric and binding
Thread for basting
Iron and ironing board
Corner and edge turner or knitting needle

Finished size is roughly:
Sleeping bag: 12 x 8in (30 x 20cm)
Fox: 10½ x 5in (26.5 x 12.75cm)

1 Fold the plain orange fat quarter in half. Mark and cut out fox shape, using the template. From plain cream, cut a 20½ x 8¾in (52 x 22cm) piece; cut a similar piece from batting. From each patterned fabric, cut two 4¾in (12cm) squares. Use the templates to cut the ear linings and face from white felt and the nose from black.

2 Cut two fox shapes from fusible fleece and trim away approximately ³/₁₆in (5mm) all around. Apply to the wrong side of the fabric pieces using a hot iron. Pin the felt shapes to the right side of one of the pieces.

3 Thread an embroidery needle with two strands of white embroidery thread and attach the felt shapes by stitching all around them in blanket stitch (see page 15).

4 Attach the felt nose in the same way, using black thread. Use the template to draw on the features with an erasable marker. Using three strands of black, embroider the eyes and paws in split stitch (see page 16).

5 Stitch the back and front together, leaving a gap of about 3in (7.5cm) on the outside of one leg. Clip corners and snip into the seam allowance on curves (see page 19).

6 Turn right side out with the aid of a corner and edge turner or similar tool. Stuff, but do not overstuff. Fold the raw edges of the gap to the inside, add more stuffing if needed, pin together, then slipstitch (see page 15).

7 Make the patchwork for the sleeping bag. With right sides together, join the squares to make two strips of five different prints. Press the seams open.

8 Join the two strips along one long side, matching the seams. Press the seam open. Place the lining on the work surface, place the batting on top, and the patchwork right side up on top of the batting. Pin and baste all around.

9 Stitch through all layers, close to the edges. This stitching will be covered by the binding. Bind one short edge using either the one-step or two-step binding method (see page 18).

10 Using a round object as a template (such as a lid from a jar), draw a curve on each corner of the unbound short edge and cut along the line you have drawn.

11 Fold over so that there are four patchwork squares on the front of the sleeping bag. Baste in place, then bind all around with the remaining bias binding using the two-step method (see page 18).

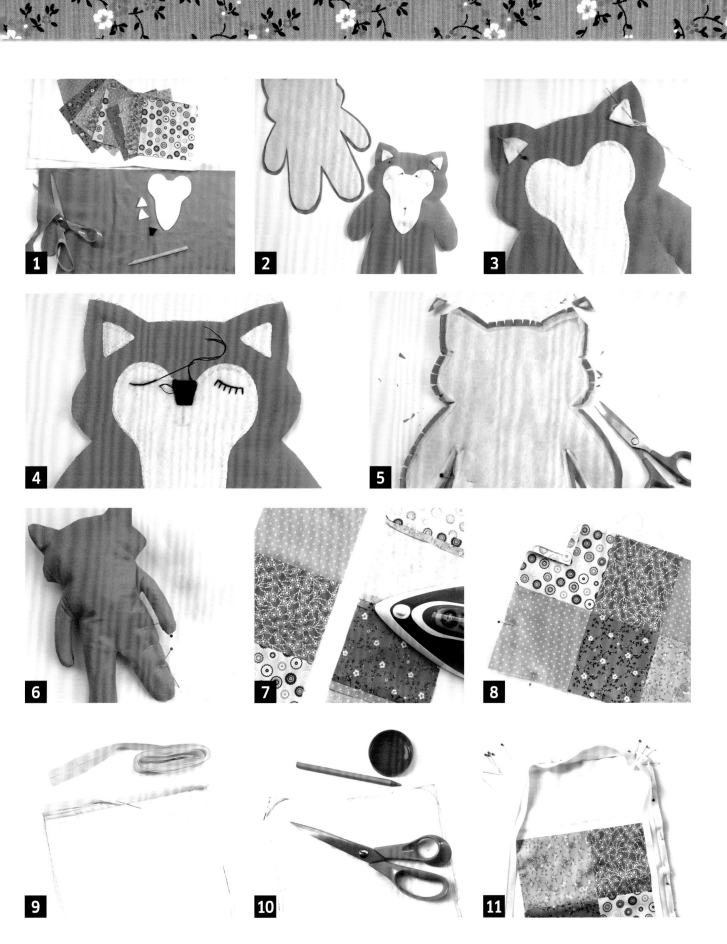

GAMES

SKITTLES

This classic indoor game helps children to develop all kinds of skills: throwing and rolling a ball, hand-eye co-ordination and counting. These skittles are smiley cats – when they are not being knocked over, they can be used for imaginative play.

Find the templates on page 140

You will need
for six skittles and one ball
2 fat quarters of printed fabric
1 fat quarter of plain fabric (pink)
12¾ x 9½in (32.5 x 24cm) of spare fabric (any kind)
Scraps of felt
Six-stranded embroidery thread in black and
    to match felt pieces
2oz (50g) plastic poly pellets (or dried lentils, beans or rice)
Polyester toy filling
Dressmaker's chalk pencil or fabric marker
Card for making templates
Pins
Dress-making scissors
General-purpose scissors
Corner and edge shaper or similar tool, such as a knitting needle
Sewing machine
Sewing needle
Embroidery (crewel) needle
Thread for basting
Thread to match fabric
Iron and ironing board

Finished size is roughly:
Each skittle: 8in (20cm) high
Ball circumference: 16in (40cm)

1 Make card templates of the cat-shaped skittle and the ear. Fold the patterned fabric in half and mark out three skittles and three ears. Mark out the facial features on the skittles. Cut out the ears but do not cut out the skittles yet.

2 Place the fabric in an embroidery hoop with the face in the centre. Cut out small circles of felt for the eyes and a triangle for the nose, matching the shapes you have drawn. Put the eyes in place and embroider a circle in the centre in satin stitch (see page 17) using an embroidery needle and two strands of black thread. Embroider lines radiating out from the centre to the edge in a colour to match the felt.

3 Fix the nose in place with small straight embroidery stitches around the edge, then with black thread go over the lines of the mouth in split stitch (see page 16). Add whiskers in split stitch. Once the embroidery is finished, cut out the skittle shapes.

4 Make the ears. Cut out twelve ear pieces from plain fabric: two ear linings for each skittle. Pair an ear lining with a patterned ear, place right sides together and stitch with a ¼in (6mm) seam, leaving the bottom edge open for turning. Snip off the point at the top. Turn right side out using a corner and edge shaper or similar tool to create a neat shape.

5 Place the ears on the front piece of the skittle, with patterned fabric uppermost. Pin and baste in place.

6 With right sides facing, place the two skittle pieces together and stitch all around the curved edge with a $^5/_{16}$in (8mm) seam, leaving a 2in (5cm) gap in one side. Stitch the straight edge on the base but leave the corners unstitched.

7 Open out the corners, line up the raw straight (open) edges and align seams. Stitch with a $^5/_{16}$in (8mm) seam. Turn right side out.

8 Make the weights. Cut two 3$^1/_8$in (8cm) squares of spare fabric for each of the skittles. Stitch around three sides with a $^5/_{16}$in (8mm) seam and clip corners.

9 Turn right side out and fill about three-quarters full with poly pellets. Turn raw edges to inside and slipstitch closed (see page 15).

10 Place the weight inside the skittle, sitting it in the base, then stuff the skittle firmly with toy filling.

11 Turn raw edges on opening to inside and slipstitch closed.

12 To make a soft ball for knocking down the skittles, cut out six segments from plain fabric, using the smaller ball template on page 140. Follow the instructions on page 24 to complete the ball.

Tip

The bean bags used for the weights at the base of the skittles can be made from any scraps of spare fabric – they're a good way of using up bits and pieces that you don't need.

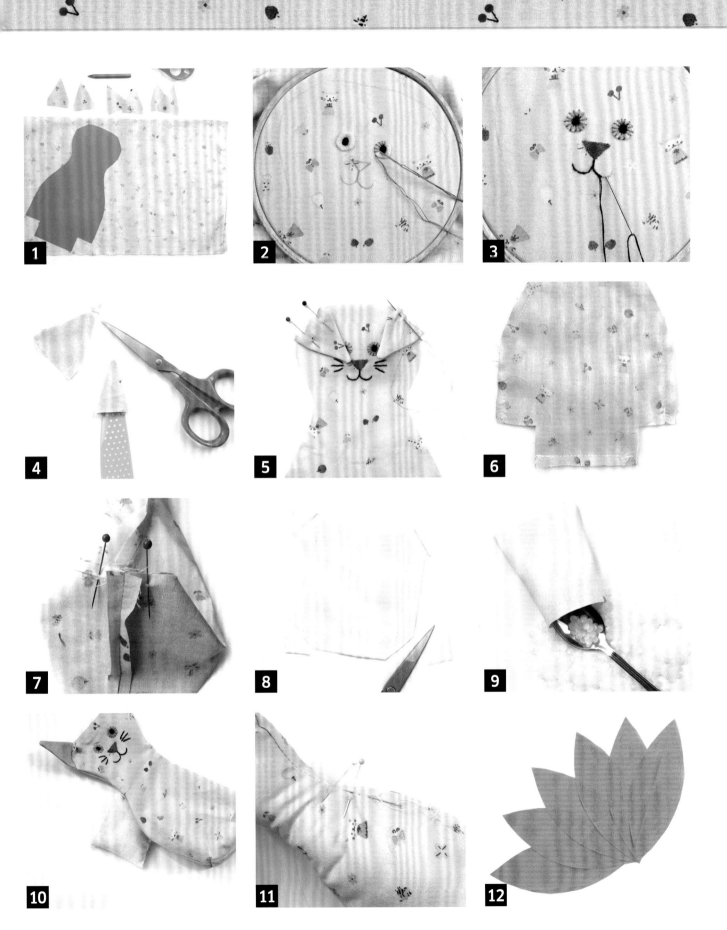

FISHING SET

Children will develop their hand-eye co-ordination by using the rod and line to 'catch' the fish and their number skills by counting how many they catch. Make as many fish as you like to populate the fabric pond: it's a great way of using up small scraps.

Find the templates on page 141

Finished size is roughly:
Fish: 6in (15cm) long
Pond diameter: 18in (45cm)

Tip
Use split rings, not jump rings. If the ribbon loop that attaches the ring to the fish is stitched firmly in place, the split ring is unlikely to become detached.

You will need
1 fat quarter of printed fabric for the pond
1 fat quarter of plain blue fabric for the pond
Scraps of plain and printed fabrics for the fish
18 x 16in (45.5 x 40.5cm) lightweight batting
Polyester toy filling
Small magnet, ¾in (2cm) diameter
Metal split rings, ³⁄₈in (1cm) diameter
1½in (4cm) of ³⁄₈in (1cm)-wide ribbon for each fish
2 x ½in (12mm) buttons for each fish
6ft (1.8m) of 1in (2.5cm)-wide bias binding in orange
15¾in (40cm) of cord
12in (30cm) wooden dowel, ⁵⁄₁₆in (8mm) in diameter
Dressmaker's chalk pencil or fabric marker
Card for making templates
Pins
Dress-making scissors
General-purpose scissors
Corner and edge shaper
Loop turner
Sewing machine
Sewing needle
Thread for basting
Thread to match fabric
Iron and ironing board

NOTE: This toy has small components and is not suitable for a child under three years of age.

1 For each fish, cut two pieces of plain fabric at least 4⅛ x 3in (10.5 x 7.5cm) and two pieces of patterned fabric at least 5½ x 4⅛in (14 x 10.5cm).

2 Join a plain and a patterned piece with a ⅜in (1cm) seam. Press the seam to one side.

3 Using the pattern piece to make a card template, draw the fish shape on the reverse of each piece of joined fabric. Make sure the line across the template is lined up with the seamline. Cut along the outline you have drawn.

4 Cut a 1½in (4cm) length of ribbon, and thread a split ring on to it. Then pin the two ends of the ribbon to the fish, at the head end. Baste in place.

5 Place two fish pieces, right sides together, matching the seams at either side. Pin, baste and stitch with a 5⁄16in (8mm) seam, leaving a 1½in (4cm) gap along one edge, for turning.

6 Clip corners and snip into seam allowance on curves. Turn right side out with the help of a corner and edge shaper or similar tool.

7 Stuff firmly but do not overstuff. Turn raw edges to inside and slipstitch folded edges together (see page 15) to close the gap.

Tip

You could make these fish for a younger child as a cuddly toy rather than as a game. Simply omit the metal ring and ribbon, and embroider the eyes instead of using buttons.

8 Sew on two buttons for eyes, taking the thread right through the head of the fish, from one side to the other. Make sure the buttons are attached firmly.

9 To make the pond, fold each of the two fat quarters in half and in half again. Use the pattern piece to make a card template. Place the two straight edges of the template on the two folds of fabric, and cut out. Cut out the same shape from lightweight batting.

10 Place the two fabric pieces wrong sides together, with the batting in between. Stitch all around, through all three layers, about ¼in (6mm) from the edge. Cut approximately 60in (1.5m) of 1in (2.5cm) bias binding and use this to bind all round the edge.

11 To make the rod, fold the remaining bias binding in half lengthways and stitch down one side with a 5⁄16in (8mm) seam. Turn right side out using a loop turner (see page 19), then insert the dowel into the fabric tube.

12 Turn under the raw edges on both ends of the rod. Insert the cord in one end, pushing about 1in (2.5cm) inside, and stitch firmly in place. Stitch the opening at the other end of the rod closed. Use the template to cut two circles of fabric. Place right sides together, pin, then stitch with a ¼in (6mm) seam, leaving a small gap for turning. Turn right side out and insert the magnet and the other end of the cord. Slipstitch the opening closed, stitching through the cord at the same time, to secure it in place.

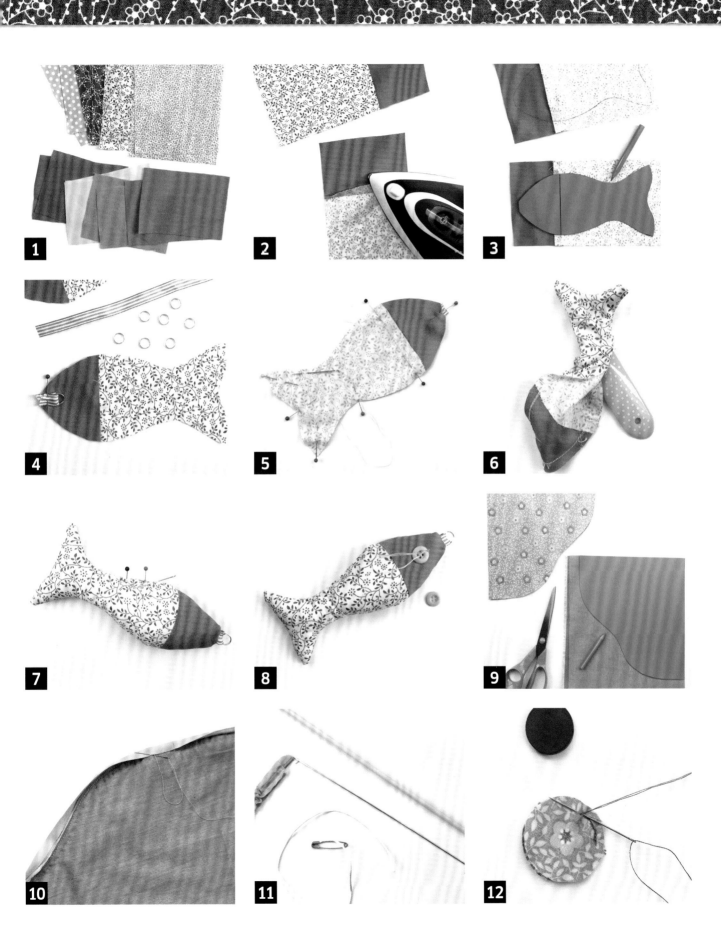

BEAN BAGS

A great way of using up scraps of material, these bean bags have a multitude of uses, from paperweights to playing games. Throw them and they stay where they land, instead of rolling away. This makes them ideal for older children learning to juggle.

You will need

Scraps of cotton fabric, at least 4¾in (12cm) square, in a variety of colours and patterns: 2 pieces for each bean bag
3oz (75g) plastic poly pellets, or dried beans or lentils, for filling
Pencil or fabric marker
Quilter's square or ruler
Pins
Dress-making scissors
Sewing machine
Sewing needle
Thread to match fabric
Knitting needle or similar tool
Iron and ironing board

NOTE: Dried peas or beans are the traditional filling for bean bags, but they are prone to sprouting if they become damp. You may prefer to use plastic poly pellets – sometimes called plastic granules, or filling beads.

Finished size is roughly:
4 x 4in (10 x 10cm) in size

1 Measure and cut out two 4¼in (12cm) squares of fabric for each bean bag.

2 Sort the fabric squares into contrasting pairs, such as one patterned and one plain or striped.

3 Stitch together around three sides of each pair with a ³⁄₈in (1cm) seam allowance.

4 Press open the top of each side seam by ¾in (2cm).

5 Match side seams and pin together, then stitch with a ³⁄₈in (1cm) seam allowance, leaving an opening in the seam of approximately 1½in (4cm).

6 Trim off corners and turn right side out, pushing out the corners with a knitting needle or similar tool.

7 Fill the bean bag through the opening in the seam, with dried beans or poly pellets. Fill approximately three-quarters full; do not overfill or the seams might burst when the bag is thrown.

8 At the opening, turn the seam allowance to the inside. Securely slipstitch the folded edges together (see page 15).

Tip

Stitch the seams as securely as possible but bear in mind that if the seams split, the filling could be a choking hazard. Therefore these bean bags are suitable only for children aged three years or older.

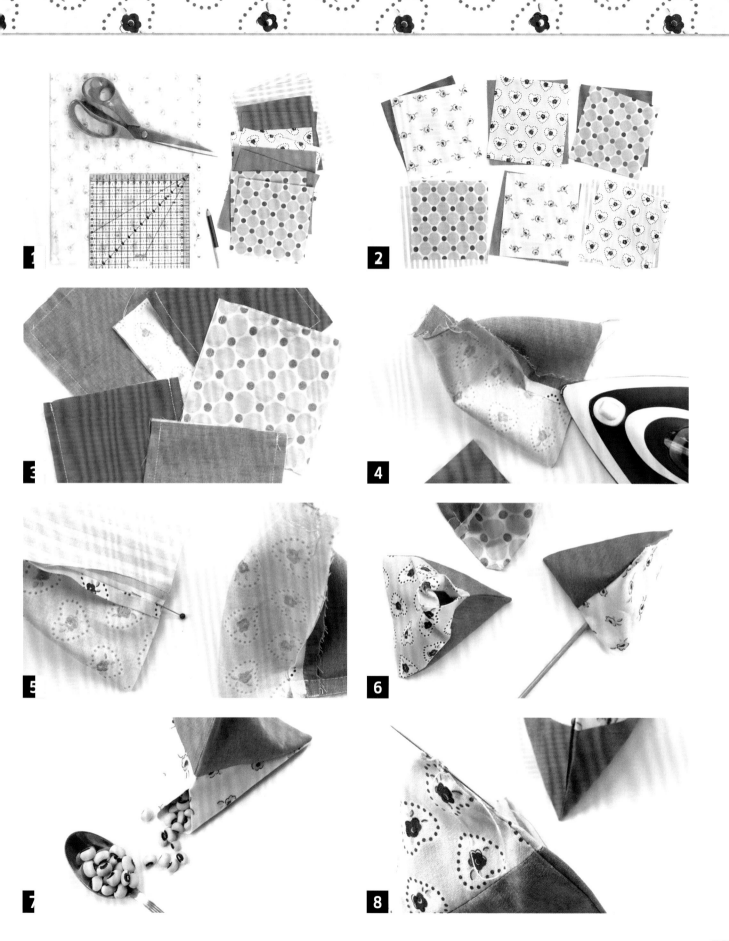

STACKING RINGS

Here is a soft version of the popular wooden or plastic stacking rings. As well as for learning to stack the rings in order of size, these soft rings can be used for throwing and catching, and for colour recognition.

Find the templates on pages 142–3

You will need
1 fat quarter of printed fabric
Pieces of plain fabric in six different colours
2 circles of spare fabric, about $3^5/_{16}$in (8cm) in diameter
20in (50cm) of fusible medium-weight interfacing
Polyester toy filling
Plastic poly pellets
Dressmaker's chalk pencil or fabric marker
Card for making templates
Pins
Pencil
Dress-making scissors
General-purpose scissors
Sewing machine
Sewing needle
Thread for basting
Thread to match fabric
Iron and ironing board

Finished size is roughly:
Approximately 10in (25cm) high and 3¾in (9.5cm) wide at the base

NOTE: The instructions for making the rings may seem confusing when you first read them but should make sense when you come to do the sewing.

1 Make card templates using the pattern pieces. Cut out the shapes: one cone shape and one small circle from patterned fabric; two rings from each of the plain fabrics; and two small circles from spare fabric.

2 For each of the pieces, apart from the two small circles, cut a piece of interfacing. Trim off about ¼in (6mm) all around, and apply to the wrong side of each fabric piece, using a hot iron.

3 Fold the cone in half, with right sides together, and stitch the side seam, leaving a gap of about 2¾in (7cm) for turning.

4 With right sides together, pin the printed circle to the base of the cone, and baste. Stitch with a ⁵⁄₁₆in (8mm) seam. Snip into the seam allowance all around (see page 19), then turn right side out.

5 To make a weight, stitch together the two circles from spare fabric with a ⁵⁄₁₆in (8mm) seam, leaving a gap of 2in (5cm) for turning. Turn right side out and fill about three-quarters full with poly pellets. Turn the raw edges to the inside and slipstitch closed (see page 15).

6 Put the weight inside the cone, placing it in the base, then stuff the cone firmly with toy filling.

7 Turn the raw edges to the inside and slipstitch the folded edges together to close the gap.

8 Place a pair of ring pieces right sides together, and stitch around the hole in the centre with a ⁵⁄₁₆in (8mm) seam. Snip into the seam allowance all around.

9 Turn right side out by pulling one of the rings through the hole in the centre. Press.

10 Make a pencil mark at any point around the edge of the outer ring and another at the same point on the other ring.

11 Take the two edges over to meet at the marked point and pin together at the mark. Place two more pins either side, holding the two layers together. Start machine stitching just below the right-hand pin and keep stitching, pulling the fabric that is trapped in the centre towards you as you do so. Remove the three pins just before that part of the ring is pulled through. Continue stitching and pulling until you reach a point 2in (5cm) from the starting point, then backstitch (see page 16) to finish the seam.

12 Turn the ring right side out through the gap, press lightly, then stuff. Turn the raw edges to the inside and slipstitch the gap closed. Repeat for the other rings.

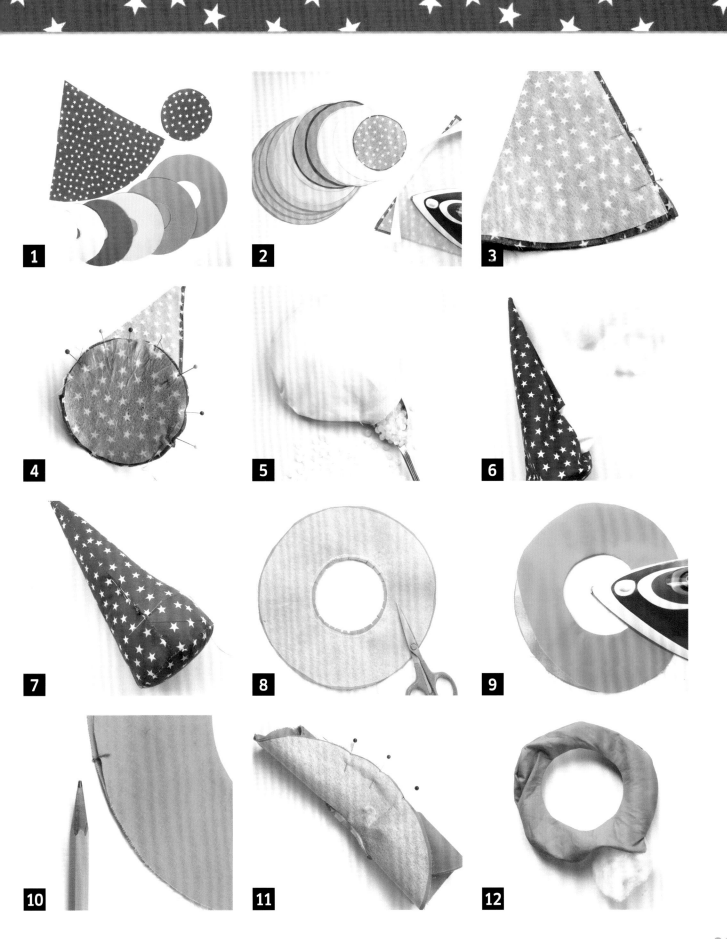

MEMORY GAME

This game is a classic. It is suitable for all ages and helps with recognition, matching and memory. Memory games made from card are easily damaged, but this stylish fabric version is washable and will last for years.

Find the template on page 143

You will need
1 fat quarter of printed fabric with pictures well spaced
1 fat quarter of printed fabric with repeating pattern
12in (30cm) square of medium-weight fusible interfacing
Piece of stiff cardboard
Dressmaker's chalk pencil or fabric marker
Pins
Dress-making scissors
Small embroidery scissors (optional)
Craft knife
Ruler
Knitting needle, or corner and edge turner, or similar tool
Sewing machine
Sewing needle
Thread to match fabric
Iron and ironing board

NOTE: You do not have to follow the exact measurements given here. Depending on the fabric you have chosen, and the size and spacing of the motifs, you may wish to make your playing pieces larger or smaller. When cutting your cardboard template, simply ensure that the outer dimensions are ¾in (2cm) larger than the inner square, to give you a ³⁄₈in (1cm) seam allowance.

Finished size is roughly:
2¹⁄₂in (6cm) square (each card)

1 Use the pattern to make a window template from cardboard. Place it on the fabric and use it as a cutting guide: make sure your chosen motif is in the centre of the window and draw around the outside of the square, to give a $^3/_8$in (1cm) seam allowance.

2 Cut out 16 squares altogether, making sure you have eight matching pairs. Cut 16 squares of the same size from the other fabric, trying to make sure that each one is identical. Then cut 16 $2^1/_4$in (6cm) squares of medium-weight fusible interfacing without a seam allowance.

3 Using a hot iron, and following the manufacturer's instructions for applying interfacing, apply a square of interfacing to the centre of the wrong side of each backing square.

4 Pin one interfaced backing square to each of the motif squares, lining up the edges neatly.

5 Stitch together around three sides with a $^3/_8$in (1cm) seam allowance. Clip corners to reduce bulk (see page 19).

6 Turn right side out, pushing out the corners with an implement such as a knitting needle or a corner and edge turner.

7 Press each piece with a hot iron, to remove any creases; turn under the seam allowance on the open edge and press.

8 Topstitch each playing piece all around, approximately $^1/_8$in (3mm) from the edge (see page 17), and press again.

Tip

Here is one way to play the game. Turn all the fabric squares picture-side down and arrange in rows. Each player takes it in turn to flip over two squares. If they match, the player takes them and has another turn. The winner is the player with the most pairs at the end of the game.

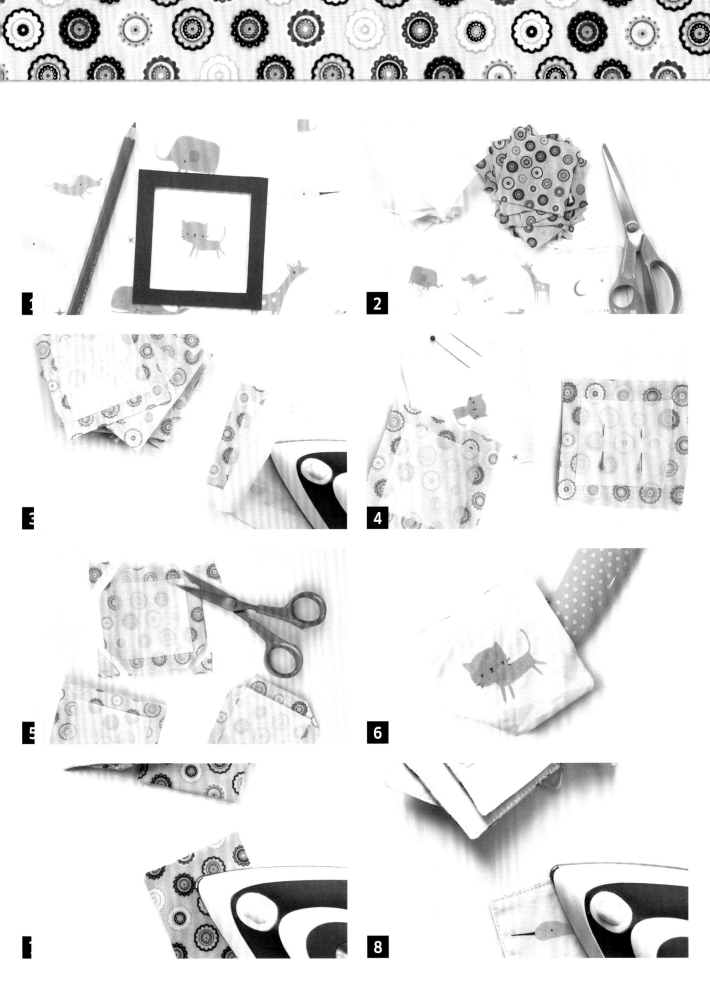

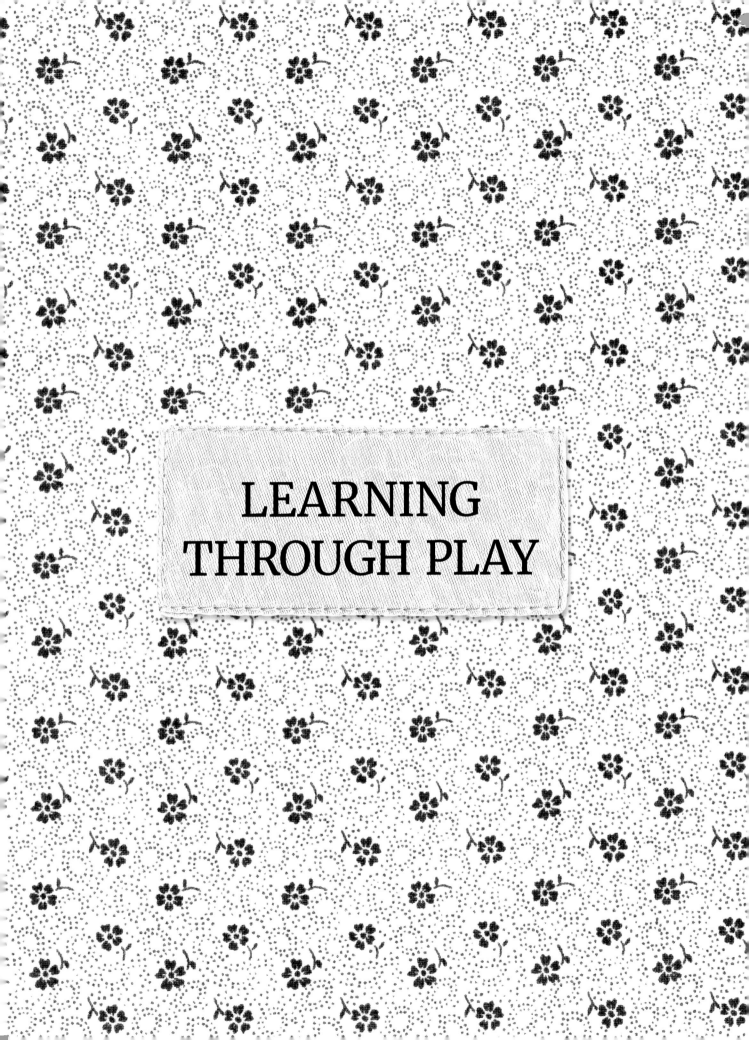

LEARNING THROUGH PLAY

ALPHABET IN A BAG

Large and easy to handle, these soft fabric letters are a great way to use up scraps of material and will help your little one learn to read and spell out words. Your child will also enjoy packing them away to carry around in the special alphabet bag.

Find the templates on page 143

You will need
1 fat quarter of plain fabric for the bag
1 fat quarter of contrast fabric for the bag lining
Scraps of various printed fabrics
7 x 12in (30cm) square pieces of felt in assorted colours
    for the backing
20in (50cm) of fusible bonding web
25 x 10in (64 x 25cm) of medium-weight fusible interfacing
2ft (60cm) of 1in (2.5cm)-wide cotton herringbone twill tape
Pencil
Pins
Dress-making scissors
Pinking shears
Small embroidery scissors
Baking paper
Sewing machine
Sewing needle
Thread to match fabric
Iron and ironing board

NOTE: Use felt that can be washed. Not all felt is washable, so you will need to check when buying, or test a piece in the washing machine before starting this project.

Finished size is roughly:
Letters: 6¼–6¾in (16–18cm) high
Bag: 10 x 9in (25 x 23cm)

1 Photocopy the letters, enlarging them by about 600 per cent until they are about 6¼–6¾in (16–18cm) high. You will need to do this in sections, or if you have a home computer and printer you can download templates from the internet and print them off. Trace each letter on to the backing paper of the fusible bonding web.

2 Cut out each letter roughly, leaving a small margin all around.

3 Place the letters on the wrong side of the fabric pieces. Using a hot iron, and following the manufacturer's instructions for applying the fusible webbing, press to fuse in place. Place a piece of baking paper in between the iron and the fabric, to prevent any adhesive being transferred on to the base plate of the iron.

4 Cut out each letter along the lines you have drawn.

5 Peel off the backing paper and place each letter on a piece of felt. The felt should be at least ¼in (6mm) larger than the letter all the way around. Press with a hot iron to fuse the fabrics together.

6 Cut out all around the letters using pinking shears.

7 For inner shapes on letters such as A, B, D, P and R, cut away the felt from these areas too. You may need to use small, pointed embroidery scissors to achieve neat corners.

8 To make the bag, cut a 23½ x 10in (60 x 25cm) rectangle from both plain fabric and contrast lining. Cut a piece of fusible interfacing 23 x 9½in (58 x 24cm) and apply to the wrong side of the plain fabric, using a hot iron.

9 Photocopy the letters A, B and C at 400 per cent so that they are approximately 3⅛in (8cm) high, then trace on to fusible bonding web. Cut out roughly and apply to the wrong side of three scraps of fabric, as before. Cut out, place on the top half of the plain fabric, and press to fuse in place.

10 Fold the fabric in half, right sides together, and stitch the side seams. Do the same with the lining. Clip the corners (see page 19) and turn the main bag right side out.

11 Press under ⅝in (1.5cm) on the top edge of the bag and the lining. Slip the lining into the bag, matching the side seams. Cut the tape into two equal lengths and sandwich the ends between the bag and the lining, on front and back, to form handles.

12 Slipstitch the folded edge of the lining neatly to the inside of the bag (see page 15).

Tip

Remember that some of the letters will appear to be back to front when you're making them. This is because they are applied to the wrong side of the fabric. They will be the right way round once they are cut out and stitched.

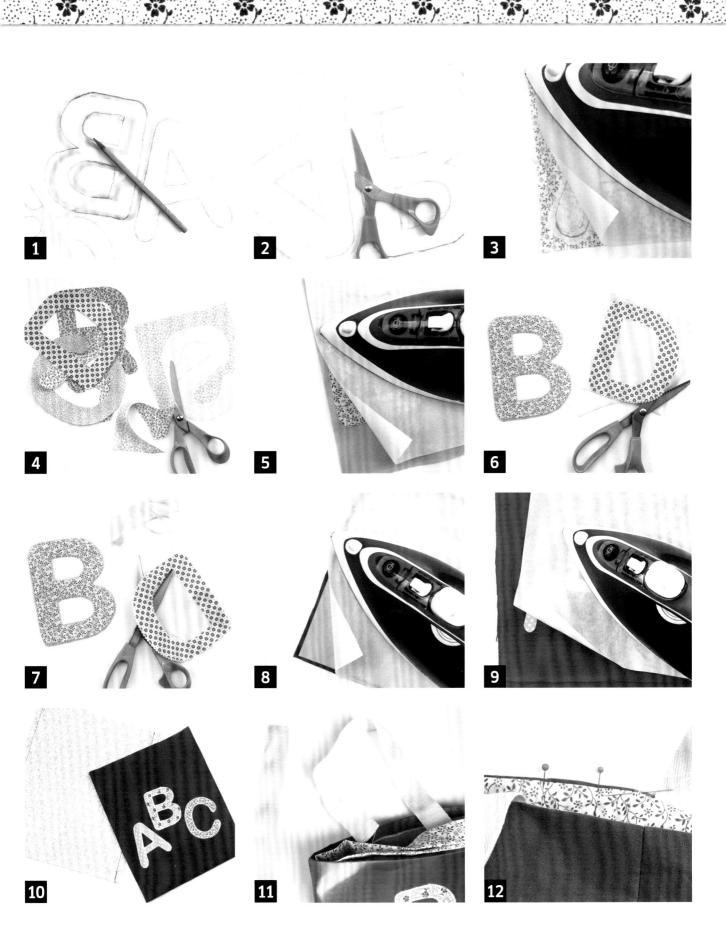

NUMBER CUBES

Soft and squishy, these foam-filled number cubes have lots of uses. Make as many as you like, with different combinations of numbers, for endless mathematical fun. Here we have added star and heart motifs as well.

Find the templates on page 144

You will need
for three balls
14¼in (36cm) squares of plain cotton fabrics
   in six different colours
Scraps of various printed fabrics
4in (10cm) foam cubes
10in (25cm) square of fusible bonding web
Pencil
Pins
Dress-making scissors
General-purpose scissors
Quilter's square or ruler
Baking paper
Sewing machine
Sewing needle
Thread for basting
Thread to match fabric
Iron and ironing board

Finished size is roughly:
4in (10cm) square per cube

Tip
You could use the letters from the bag project on page 88 to make alphabet cubes instead.

1 Using a quilter's square or ruler, cut six 4¾in (12cm) squares of plain cotton fabric for each cube.

2 Using the templates, trace the numbers and the star and heart on to the backing paper of the fusible web. The numbers will be reversed – though the eight and the zero will appear the same. Arrange the numbers in such a way that you waste as little of the webbing material as possible, but make sure there is some space between them.

3 Cut out each number roughly, with a small margin all around.

4 Place the cut-out numbers, and the star and heart, adhesive-side down on the wrong side of the printed fabric scraps. Press with a hot iron. Place a piece of baking paper in between the iron and the fabric, to prevent any adhesive being transferred on to the base plate of the iron.

5 Cut out the numbers and motifs along the lines.

6 Peel off the backing paper from each letter and motif, and place each one centrally on a fabric square. Press.

7 Stitch around each number with a machine zigzag stitch using a matching or toning thread. Press with a hot iron.

8 Pin four squares together in a row, as shown. Baste.

9 Stitch with a ⅜in (1cm) seam allowance, beginning and ending each seam ⅜in (1cm) from top and bottom edges. Press seams open.

10 Pin a square to the bottom of the joined squares and another to the top. On one, stitch around all four sides; on the other, stitch around two sides only.

11 Clip the corners (see page 19) and turn right side out. Insert a foam cube.

12 Turn the raw edges to the inside on the open edges, pin together, then slipstitch the gap closed (see page 15). Repeat for the other cubes.

Tip

For a neat finish, start and finish the zigzag stitch at the same point. Cut threads, leaving a tail of about 3in (7.5cm), then pull them to the wrong side and tie firmly together.

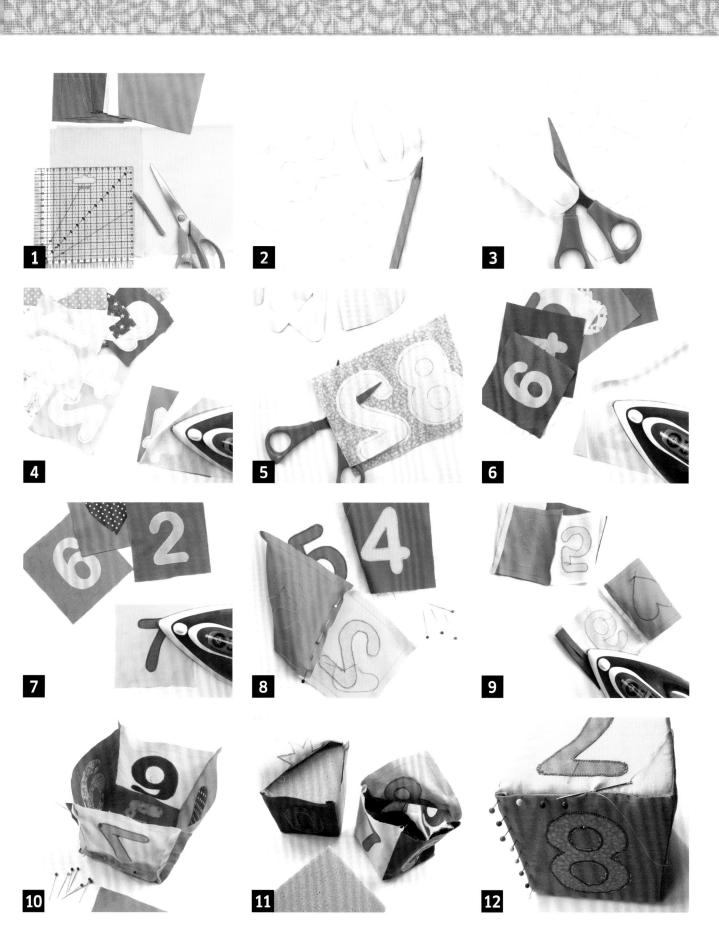

SUN PILLOW

This bright and cheerful disc of sunshine will help your child with colour and shape recognition. Different shapes are appliquéd on to the pillow to create a smiley face, and the colourful ribbon tags provide another texture to feel.

Find the templates on page 144

You will need
1 fat quarter of plain yellow fabric
Scraps of various printed fabrics
10in (25cm) of $^5\!/_8$in (1.5cm)–wide cotton tape or ribbon in each of eight colours
10in (25cm) square of medium–weight fusible interfacing
8 x 6in (20 x 15cm) of fusible bonding web
Polyester toy filling
Pencil or fabric marker
Pins
Dress–making scissors
General–purpose scissors
Sewing machine
Sewing needle
Thread for basting
Thread to match fabric
Iron and ironing board

NOTE: Light– and medium–weight plain fabric will benefit from being backed with interfacing, but if you choose a slightly heavier fabric, you may not need to interface it.

Finished size is roughly:
10in (25cm) diameter

1 Fold the fat quarter of yellow fabric in half. Place a dinner plate or similar round object approximately 10¾in (27cm) in diameter on the double thickness of fabric and draw around the perimeter using a pencil or other fabric marker.

2 Pin the two layers together and cut out the circles of fabric. Cut out two circles of medium-weight fusible interfacing, 10in (25cm) in diameter, and apply one to the wrong side of each fabric circle, using a hot iron.

3 Using the templates, trace the shapes for the face on to the paper backing of the fusible web. Cut around each shape roughly, leaving a small margin all around.

4 Place the shapes on the wrong side of the fabric scraps. Using a hot iron, and following the manufacturer's instructions for applying the fusible web, press to fuse in place.

5 Cut out each shape along the lines you have drawn. Peel off the backing paper and place the shapes on one of the yellow circles. When you are happy with the arrangement, press with a hot iron to fuse the fabric shapes in place. Place a piece of baking paper in between the iron and the fabric, to prevent any adhesive being transferred on to the base plate of the iron.

6 Using a close machine zigzag stitch, and thread colours to match the various fabrics, outline each shape (see page 17). To neaten thread ends and prevent unravelling, pull each one to the wrong side and knot together firmly before trimming.

7 Cut sixteen 4¾in (12cm) lengths of tape. Fold each one in half to make a loop. Lining up cut edges with the edge of the fabric circle, position each ribbon around the perimeter, evenly spaced. (To do this, start by positioning a fabric loop at the top, bottom and side points of the circle to divide it into four sections. Position three more ribbons in each of these sections to divide the circle into 16.) Pin each ribbon in place, baste, then remove the pins.

8 Place the two circles, right sides together, and pin all around. Stitch, with a ½in (12mm) seam allowance, leaving a gap of about 5in (12.75cm) for turning.

9 Snip into the seam allowance all around. Turn right side out and turn seam allowance on opening to inside. Press.

10 Stuff the pillow with polyester toy filling. Do not add too much filling – just enough to create a soft pillow.

11 Slipstitch the folded edges together (see page 15) using matching thread.

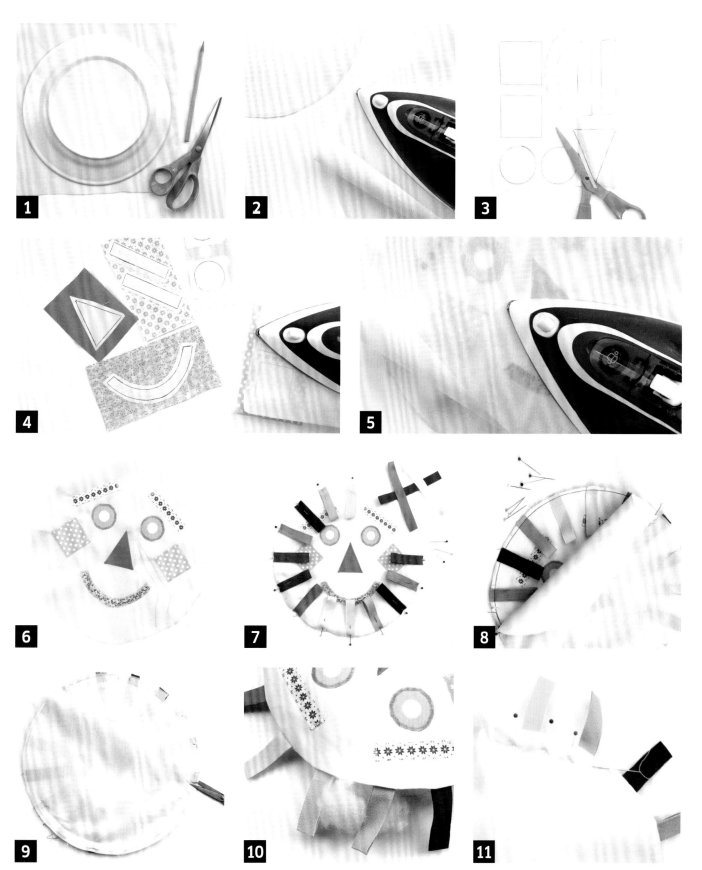

RAG BOOK

Using colour and texture, the pages of this rag book are visually stimulating and tactile. The butterfly wings are attached under the body of the butterfly, leaving them free to flap. Filled with crinkle fabric, they create a sensory rustling sound when touched.

Find the templates on page 145

NOTES: Raid your scraps bag for various fabrics suitable for appliqué. You will need plain and printed cottons – including brown print for the trees and striped fabric for the laundry basket – and textured fabrics such as silks and velvets.

WARNING: This book contains small parts and is suitable only for children aged three years and over.

Finished size is roughly:
9¹/₂in (24cm) square when closed

You will need
3 fat quarters of plain cotton fabric
1 fat quarter of printed cotton fabric
8in (20cm) square of brown printed cotton fabric
5in (12.75cm) square of both green cotton and striped fabric
Scraps of various fabrics, including velvet, for appliqué
5¹/₂ x 19in (14 x 48cm) piece of sheer fabric for the water
16in (40cm) square of fusible bonding web
20in (50cm) of medium-weight fusible interfacing
4³/₈in (11cm)-square pieces of felt in cream, red, orange, white and beige
8in (20cm) square of crinkle fabric
8in (20cm) length of string
3 mini clothes pegs
8in (20cm) of ribbon and braid
60in (1.5m) of 1in (2.5cm)-wide plain bias binding
60in (1.5m) of 1in (2.5cm)-wide patterned bias binding
Pencil or erasable marker
Six-stranded embroidery thread in colours to match fabrics
Polyester toy stuffing
Pins
Dress-making scissors and general-purpose scissors
Quilter's square or ruler
Sewing machine
Sewing needle
Embroidery (crewel) needle
Thread to match fabric and felt
Thread for basting
Iron and ironing board

1 Cut four rectangles of different fabrics measuring 19 x 9½in (48 x 24cm), for the pages. Cut four pieces of medium-weight fusible interfacing, each measuring 18½ x 9in (47 x 23cm) and apply to the wrong side of each fabric rectangle, using a hot iron. Place a piece of baking paper in between the iron and the fabric, to prevent any adhesive being transferred on to the base plate of the iron.

2 Using the templates, trace appliqué shapes on to the paper backing of fusible bonding web: the duck; eight petal shapes for the duck wing, owl wing and flower petals; three tree trunks (including one in reverse); two tree tops; one owl and one baby owl; one lion head; one butterfly body; one strip of grass and one circle for the flower centre. Cut out the shapes, leaving a small margin around each one, ready to apply to the various fabrics.

3 Cut out wing pieces: two from brown printed cotton fabric, for the owl; and eight from silky fabric and four from crinkle fabric, for the butterfly. Place pairs with right sides together. On each butterfly wing, place a crinkle wing on top. Stitch all around curved edges on each wing, leaving the short straight edge unstitched. Snip into the seam allowance on curves and turn each wing right side out (see page 19). Press.

4 For pages 1 and 6, take one of the rectangles from step 1 and stitch the owl wing on the left-hand side and the butterfly wings on the right-hand side. On page 1, assemble the pieces so that the owls are sitting on the branch, with the baby owl underneath the big owl's wing, then stitch in place. On page 6, bond the fusible bonding web of the butterfly body to the wrong side of a scrap of velvet. Cut out along the outline, peel off the backing paper, and place the butterfly body in the centre of the wings, covering the raw edges. Fuse in place.

5 For pages 3 and 4, bond the duck shape and one of the petal shapes to the wrong side of velvet scraps. Cut out along the outlines, peel off the backing paper, and place the duck on the left-hand side, with the wing on top. Fuse in place with a hot iron. Hem one long edge of the sheer fabric, then baste in place on the bottom half of the rectangle, to form water.

6 For page 4, cut the three frog pieces from green felt. Place the zip behind the slit in the frog's head and stitch in place. Place the frog pieces on the page and stitch in place.

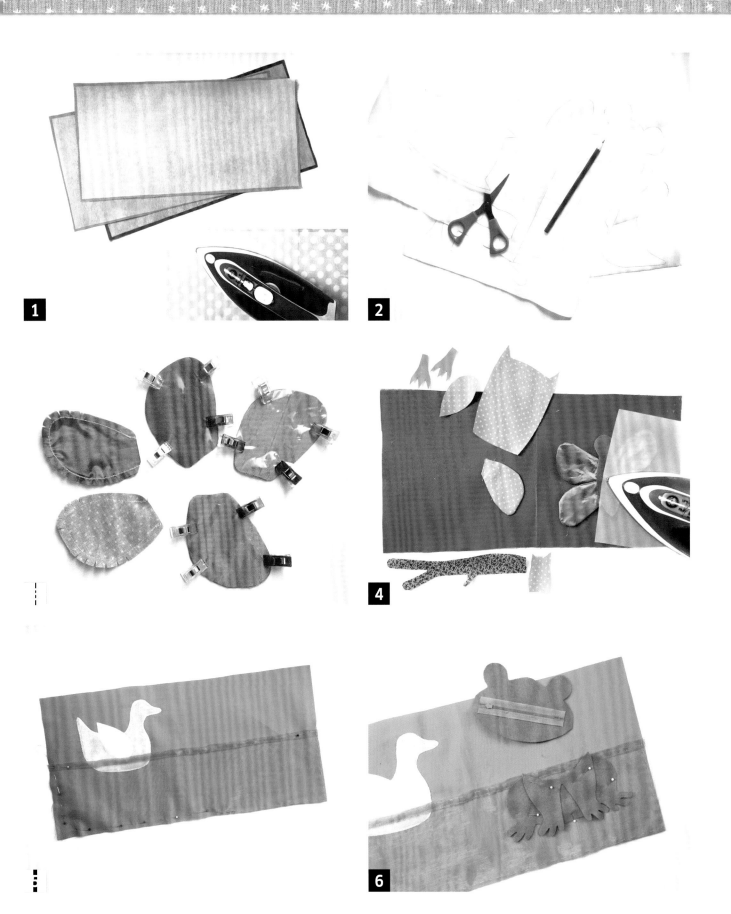

7 For pages 2 and 5, fuse two tree-trunk shapes to brown printed cotton and the grass strip to green cotton fabric. Place these components on the right-hand side of the background rectangle. Thread the string through the springs of the pegs. Loop and knot the ends of the string and place over the branches, then fuse in place. Cut two basket shapes from striped fabric and stitch together with a ¼in (6mm) seam, leaving the bottom edge unstitched, then turn right side out. Line up the raw edge with the bottom of the page and stitch the basket in place, leaving the top edge open.

8 On the other half of page 5, use the flower centre template to mark out a circle in the centre. Cut lengths of ribbon and braid, each approximately 4in (10cm) long, and place with one end inside the circle, radiating outwards. Stitch in place within the circle. Apply the lion head traced in step 2 to the wrong side of a scrap of textured fabric. Cut out and fuse to the circle, covering the stitched ribbon ends. Trim the other ends of the ribbon and braid to make them equal.

9 For the front cover, bond the remaining petal shapes and the circle to various different textured fabric scraps. Position these and fuse in place with a hot iron.

10 Stitch around the flower petals and centre using a close machine zigzag stitch. On all the other pages, stitch around each of the appliqué shapes in a similar way.

11 Cut out facial features and other details from coloured felt. Pin these in place on the various pages, and hand stitch to secure each one, using an embroidery needle and embroidery thread to match fabrics. Use satin stitch (see page 17) to sew antennae for the butterfly. Cut out several fish shapes and tuck these behind the sheer fabric on page 3, ready to be transferred to the frog's unzipped mouth on page 4. Cut out several sock shapes and place these in the washing basket on page 2, ready to be pegged on to the line.

12 Place pages 2 and 5 back to back with pages 3 and 4. Baste all around, close to the edges, then bind with bias binding, starting and finishing in the centre, overlapping the ends neatly. Do the same with pages 1 and 6 and the cover. Place the two sections on top of each other, with pages 3 and 4 uppermost, and the section with the cover face down. Stitch down the centre, through all thicknesses, to join the pages together.

Tip

Use a close zigzag machine stitch in step 10 to stitch the edges of the bonded fabric shapes to the pages. The bonding web secures the shapes to the backing fabric, and the stitching ensures that the edges are firmly held down.

IMAGINATIVE PLAY

MONKEY HAND PUPPET

Hand puppets provide hours of fun for little ones. This one is perfect for small hands, with a soft, comfortable lining. Your child will enjoy putting on a show, telling stories and making animal noises with this cheeky monkey puppet.

Find the templates on page 146

WARNING: This toy contains small parts and is suitable only for children aged three years and over.

You will need
1 fat quarter of printed cotton fabric in beige
1 fat quarter of printed cotton fabric in blue
1 fat quarter of plain cotton fabric in beige
Scraps of tan, beige, black and white felt
12 x 10in (30 x 25cm) of fusible fleece
Two buttons
Dressmaker's chalk pencil or erasable marker
Six-stranded embroidery thread to match felt
Polyester toy stuffing
Pins
Dress-making scissors
General-purpose scissors
Quilter's square or ruler
Baking paper
Sewing machine
Sewing needle
Embroidery (crewel) needle
Thread to match fabric
Thread for basting
Iron and ironing board

Finished size is roughly:
12in (30cm) long, not including tail

1 Using the templates, from beige printed fabric, cut two upper body pieces, two heads, four ears and two tails. From blue printed fabric, cut four straps and two rectangles measuring $6\frac{1}{8}$ x $5\frac{1}{2}$in (15.5 x 14cm). From plain beige fabric, cut two body linings. From tan felt, cut one muzzle and two paws; from beige felt, cut two ear linings.

2 With right sides together, stitch two pairs of straps all around with a $\frac{1}{4}$in (6mm) seam, leaving the short straight ends unstitched. Snip into the seam allowance on curves (see page 19) and turn right side out. Press. Topstitch all around, $\frac{1}{8}$in (3mm) from edge (see page 17).

3 Pin and baste the straps to one of the rectangles as shown. Join this blue rectangle to one upper body piece and the other to the other upper body piece, with a $\frac{5}{16}$in (8mm) seam, giving you two main body pieces, back and front. Press seams open.

4 Use the body template to cut two pieces of fusible fleece and trim off $\frac{3}{16}$in (5mm) all around. Place one piece on the wrong side of the back and front and press to fuse in place, using a piece of baking paper to protect the base plate of the iron. Cut four ear shapes from fusible fleece, trim off $\frac{3}{16}$in (5mm) all around, and apply to the ear pieces.

5 Pin the paws and ear linings in place and attach with blanket stitch (see page 15), using two strands of matching embroidery thread.

6 With right sides together, stitch the front and back bodies together. Do the same with the plain fabric pieces, to make the body lining. Snip into the seam allowance on curves. Turn the main body right side out.

7 Make the tail in the same way as the straps. Turn right side out and stuff lightly, leaving the top 1in (2.5cm) unstuffed. Slip the lining inside the body and turn under $\frac{3}{8}$in (1cm) on both raw edges. Place the open end of the tail between the layers at the centre back, slipstitch folded edges together (see page 15), then topstitch all round.

8 Cut two pieces of fusible fleece slightly smaller than the head and fuse to each head piece. On one head piece, pin the muzzle in place Thread an embroidery needle with two strands of embroidery thread to match the muzzle and stitch all around with blanket stitch. Cut two eyes from black felt and attach them with blanket stitch too. Cut two tiny circles of white felt and stitch in place as highlights on the eyes. Cut small strips of black felt for the nostrils and mouth and stitch these in place.

9 Stitch the ears with a $\frac{1}{4}$in (6mm) seam allowance and turn right side out. Pin and baste to the sides of the head front. Stitch the head pieces together with a $\frac{5}{16}$in (8mm) seam.

10 Stuff the head. Turn under $\frac{3}{8}$in (1cm) on the neck opening and slip over the top of the body, with most of the stuffing at the front. Slipstitch the folded edge to the body with small, neat, firm stitches.

11 Flip the straps over to the front and stitch in place, then stitch a button on each one.

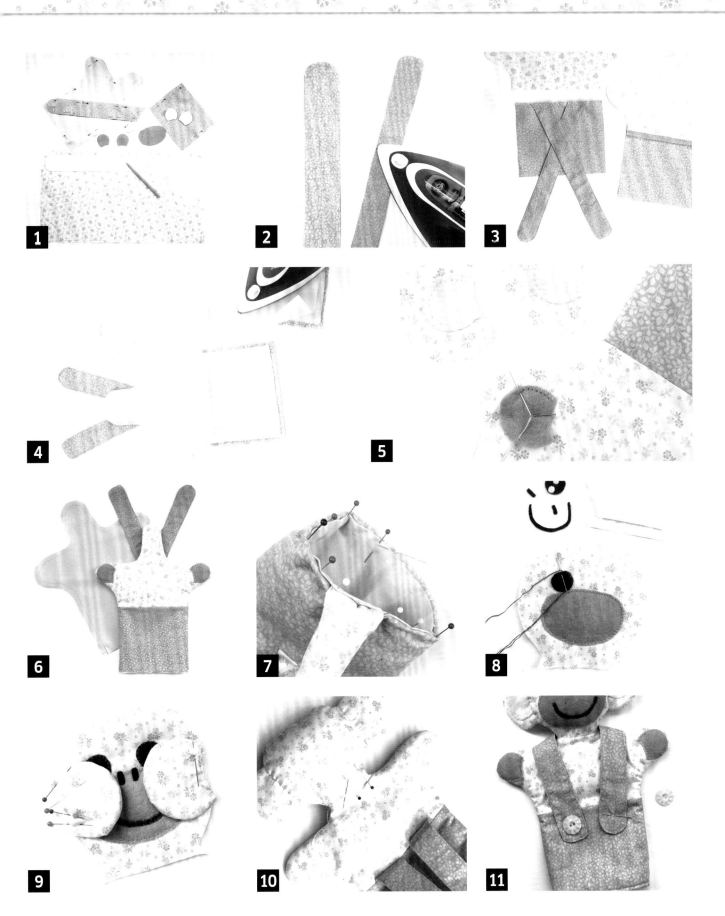

RAG DOLL

This fabric doll is smiley and huggable. She can be dressed in her wrapover dress and matching knickers, or left as she is. Either way, your little one will think she's adorable, and she's bound to become a constant companion.

Find the templates on page 147

You will need
1 fat quarter of plain fabric in preferred skin colour
1 fat quarter of printed fabric for clothes
11 x 7in (28 x 18cm) felt in preferred hair colour
14in (35.5cm) of ¼in (6mm)–wide (35.5 x 6mm) elastic
20in (51cm) of ⅝in (1.5cm)–wide bias binding
Two press studs
Chalk pencil or erasable marker
Embroidery hoop
Six-stranded embroidery thread in preferred colours
    for features
Pins
Dress-making scissors
General-purpose scissors
Quilter's square or ruler
Sewing machine
Sewing needle
Embroidery (crewel) needle
Thread for basting
Thread to match fabric
Iron and ironing board
Safety pin for threading elastic

Finished size is roughly:
13½in (34cm) long

NOTE: The dress is fastened with press fasteners.
Make sure these are sewn on securely if the doll is to be given to a child under three years, to prevent a choking hazard.

1 Fold the plain fabric fat quarter in half and use the templates to draw the pattern pieces: head and body piece with facial features, two arms and two legs. Pin the layers together and cut out the arms and legs – but don't cut out the head and body yet.

2 Place the head and body piece of the doll in an embroidery hoop, with the face in the centre. Thread an embroidery needle with two strands of black embroidery thread and embroider the pupils of the eyes in satin stitch (see page 17). With green thread – or the colour of your choice – embroider the rest of the eye in satin stitch, with the stitches radiating out from the centre. Outline the eyes and eyelashes in split stitch (see page 16). For the nose and mouth, embroider lines of backstitch (see page 16), then go over either side of these lines in satin stitch to fill them out a bit. Do the same with the eyebrows.

3 Remove the head and body piece from the embroidery hoop. Place pairs of shapes together. Pin, baste and stitch. In each case, leave the lower straight edge open. Snip corners and snip into the seam allowance on curved edges (see page 19).

4 Turn legs right side out and stuff, leaving the top ½in (1.25cm) unfilled. Line up seams and baste top edges together. Turn the head and body right side out and pin legs to bottom edge of back body with feet facing forwards as shown. Stitch ⁵⁄₁₆in (8mm) from raw edge.

5 Fold legs downwards. Stuff body and head; do not overstuff. Tuck under ⁵⁄₁₆in (8mm) on lower edge. Then pin, baste and stitch across, about ⅛in (3mm) from the folded edges.

6 Stuff arms, leaving the top ½in (1.25cm) unfilled. Tuck under ⁵⁄₁₆in (8mm) on raw edges, line up seams, and slipstitch folded edges together (see page 15). Pin arm to body, matching seams, and slipstitch top of arm securely to body.

7 Cut the two hair pieces from brown felt (or other colour chosen). On the back piece, stitch the two edges of the 'V' shape together. Place back and front pieces right sides together and stitch all around with a ⁵⁄₁₆in (8mm) seam.

8 Turn the hair right side out and slip on to head. Thread a needle with two strands of matching embroidery thread and stitch in place with small, neat stitches.

9 To make matching knickers, cut a rectangle of printed fabric measuring 11 x 4⅛in (28 x 10.5cm). Hem both long edges by turning ³⁄₁₆in (5mm) to wrong side, then ⅜in (1cm). Press, then stitch close to edge. Cut two 7in (18cm) lengths of elastic and thread these through the channels using a safety pin. Stitch across both ends to hold the elastic in place.

10 Join the two short ends to form a ring. Press the seam open. Flatten the piece, placing the seam in the centre. Oversew the two edges together at the centre for about ½in (1.25cm).

11 For the dress, cut out one back and two front pieces. Stitch together at sides and shoulders with a ⁵⁄₁₆in (8mm) seam allowance. Press seams open.

12 Hem the lower edge and the two front edges. Use bias binding to bind the raw edges on the armholes and neckline (see page 18). Stitch press studs in place on the front, to fasten.

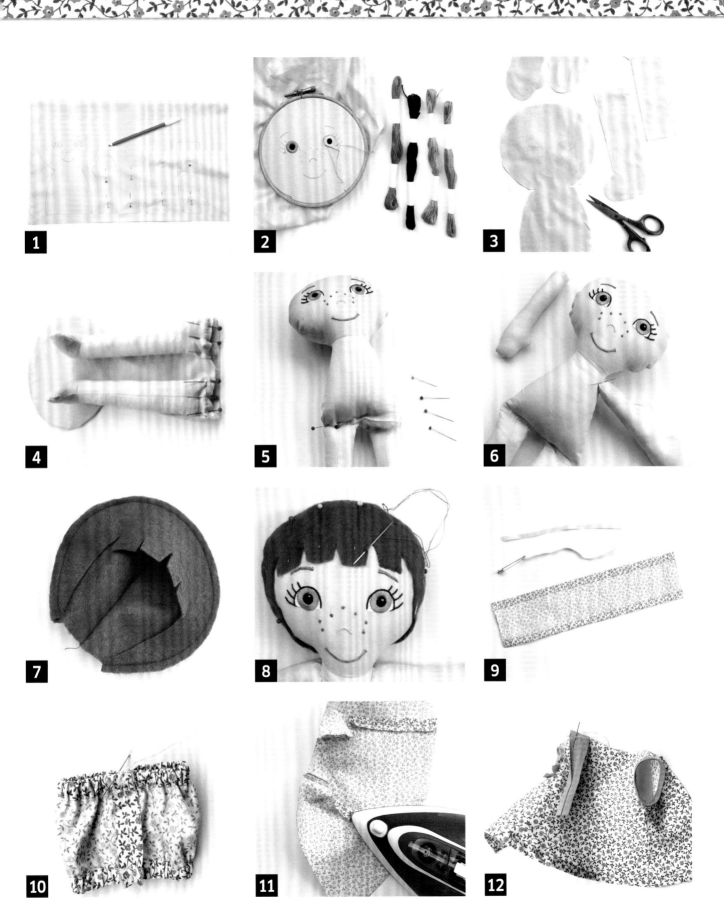

FRUITS

Fabric fruits are great for playing at shopping or preparing food, or for a teddy bears' picnic. These delightful fruits can be included in the picnic on page 124, and the apple could even double as a ball for playing skittles.

Find the templates on page 148

You will need
1 fat quarter of printed cotton fabric in pink
1 fat quarter of printed cotton fabric in green
Scraps of printed cotton in red with white spots, and brown
Scraps of green felt
Chalk pencil or erasable marker
Polyester toy stuffing
Pins
Dress-making scissors
General-purpose scissors
Small scissors
Quilter's square or ruler
Loop turner
Sewing machine
Sewing needle
Thread to match fabric and felt
Iron and ironing board

Finished size is roughly:
Apple: 3¾in (9.5cm) long
Pear: 4½in (11.5cm) long
Strawberry: 2in (5cm) long

1 For the apple and pear, use the templates to cut five apple segments from pink fabric and four pear segments from green fabric. Cut one strip of brown fabric measuring 4³⁄₈ x 1³⁄₈in (11 x 3.5cm) for both stalks.

2 To make the stalks, fold the strip in half lengthways with right sides together and stitch with a ⁵⁄₁₆in (8mm) seam. Turn right side out using a loop turner (see page 19).

3 Cut the piece in half. On each one, tuck in the raw edge on one end, then fold the piece in half lengthways and oversew the edges together (see page 15). To create a curved stem, pull up the thread carefully to gather the stitched edge slightly.

4 Stitch the open end of the stalk to the top end of one of the segments, for both the apple and the pear.

5 With right sides facing, stitch the first two segments together, for the pear (shown in the picture) and the apple. Stitch along the curved edge with a ⁵⁄₁₆in (8mm) seam, starting and ending the seam ⁵⁄₁₆in (8mm) from the edge. Make sure you backstitch at the beginning and end of the seam so that it doesn't come undone.

6 Join the remaining segments. When stitching the last seam, which joins the two remaining raw edges, leave a gap of approximately 4in (10cm) in the centre of the seam, for turning.

7 Snip into the seam allowance on all curved seams (see page 19), then turn right side out. Stuff. Turn under ⁵⁄₁₆in (8mm) on the opening, pin the folded edges together, then slipstitch to close the gap (see page 15).

8 For each strawberry, cut two shapes from red spotted fabric and one rectangle measuring 1¼ x ⁵⁄₈in (3 x 1.5cm) from green felt. Roll up the felt lengthways and secure the long edge with small stitches, then stitch this stalk to one of the strawberry pieces.

9 Stitch the two halves of the strawberry together with a ⁵⁄₁₆in (8mm) seam, leaving a gap of about 1in (2.5cm) on one side, for turning. Snip into the seam allowance on curves and turn right side out.

10 Add stuffing, turn raw edges to inside and slipstitch the opening closed. For each strawberry, cut a calyx shape from green felt. Cut a small hole in the centre with small scissors. Slip over the stalk and stitch in place, to secure it.

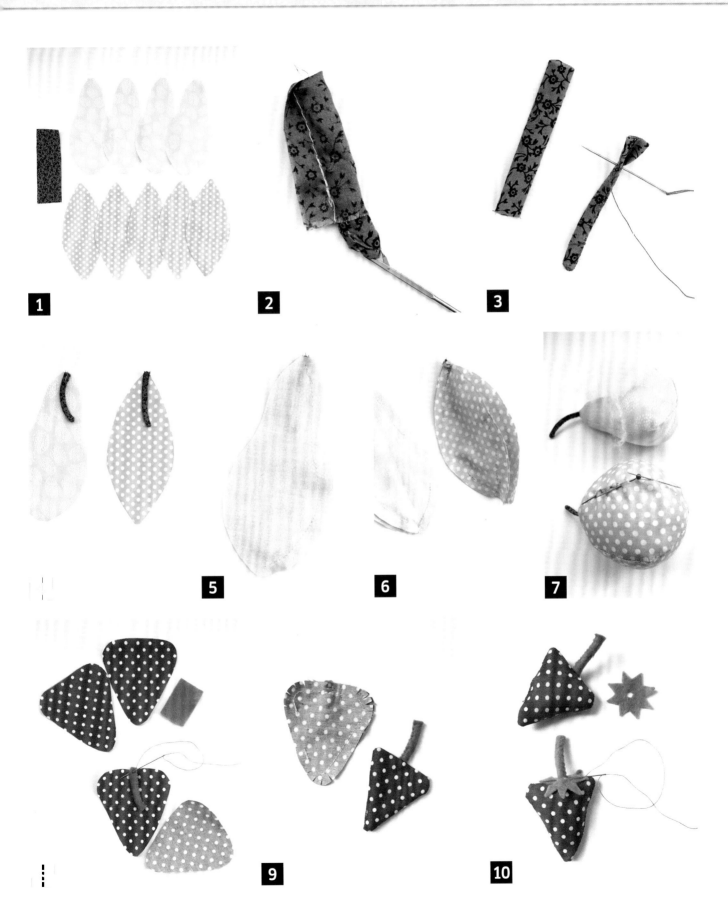

VEGETABLES

Here are some colourful vegetables to add to your child's collection – ideal for setting up a greengrocer's shop or market stall, or pretending to cook. Make a few extra salad leaves and include these in the sandwich fillings for the picnic on page 124.

Find the templates on page 148

You will need
1 fat quarter of plain cotton fabric in orange
1 fat quarter of plain cotton fabric in purple
4in (10cm) square pieces of green felt
Chalk pencil or erasable marker
Polyester toy stuffing
Pins
Dress-making scissors
General-purpose scissors
Quilter's square or ruler
Sewing machine
Sewing needle
Thread to match fabric and felt
Iron and ironing board

Finished sizes roughly:
Aubergine: 4¾in (12cm) long
Carrot: 6¼in (15.75cm) long
Salad leaf: 4in (10cm) long

1 For each carrot, use the template to cut one carrot piece from orange fabric. Fold it in half, right sides together, and stitch together down the long edge with a $^5/_{16}$in (8mm) seam allowance. Leave the top open.

2 Turn each carrot right sides out and add stuffing; do not overstuff, and leave the top 1in (2.5cm) unstuffed.

3 Fold under $^5/_{16}$in (8mm) on the top edge. Stitch a gathering (running) stitch all around the folded edge.

4 Pull up the thread to tighten the gathering stitches and close the gap, then fasten off.

5 For the aubergine, use the template to cut out four shapes from purple fabric.

6 Stitch the first two segments together: stitch along the curved edge with a $^5/_{16}$in (8mm) seam. Join the other two together, then join the two pairs. When stitching the last seam, leave a gap of approximately 4in (10cm) in the centre of the seam, for turning.

7 Snip into the seam allowance on all curved seams, then turn right side out (see page 19). Stuff. Turn under $^5/_{16}$in (8mm) on the opening, pin the folded edges together, then slipstitch to close the gap (see page 15).

8 Cut out the calyx shape from green felt, using the template. Cut a small circle for each carrot and aubergine, using the template. Stitch the calyx to the top end of the aubergine and stitch a small circle in the centre of this calyx. Stitch a circle to the top end of each carrot, to cover the small hole.

9 For each salad leaf, use the template to cut the leaf shape from green felt. Fold along the centre and hand stitch through the fold using running stitch to create the central leaf vein. Make additional folds, from the centre vein to the edge of the leaf, and stitch again to make the leaf veins.

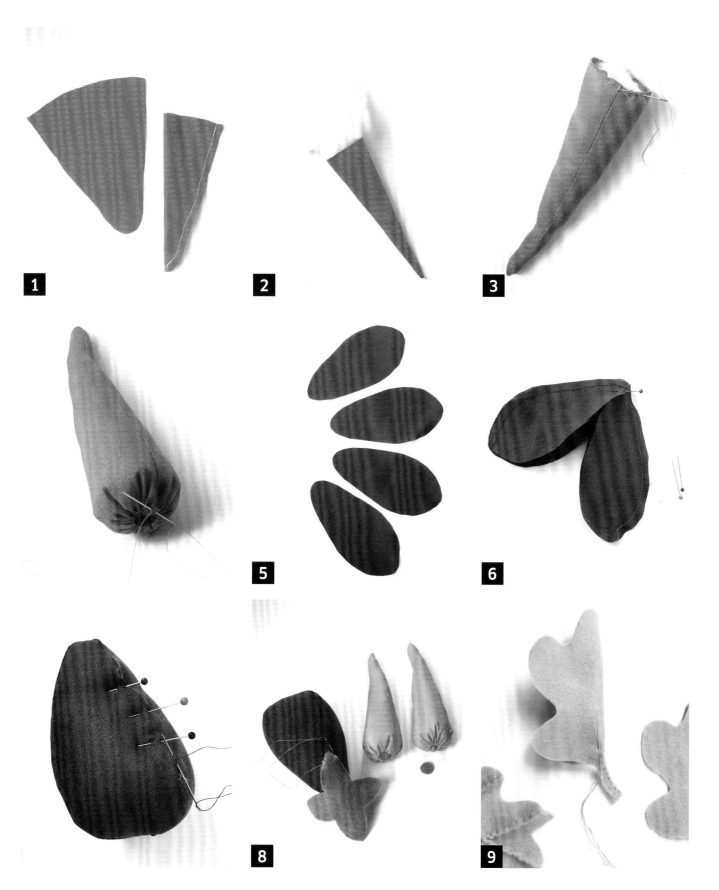

PICNIC

This picnic comes in its own handy bag. It contains crisps, tortilla chips and a sandwich with a choice of fillings. Add the salad leaves from page 120 and the apple, pear and strawberries from page 116 for a healthy packed lunch!

Find the templates on pages 148–9

NOTE: In step 3, you cut four strips of brown felt: two for each bread crust. This assumes that you are using felt squares. If you have a larger piece of felt, you may need to cut only one long strip for each slice of bread.

Finished sizes roughly:
Sandwich: 4in (10cm) square
Crisp packet: 5½ x 4½in (14 x 11.5cm)
Bag: 8 x 5½ x 5in (20 x 14 x 12.75cm)

You will need
1 fat quarter of printed cotton fabric for the bag
1 fat quarter of plain cotton fabric for the lining
6½ x 5¼in (16.5 x 13cm) crinkle fabric
12 x 5¼in (30 x 13cm) craft foam
6 x 4in (15 x 10cm) bonding web
30in (76cm) of ½in (1.25cm)-wide cotton tape or ribbon for the bag handles
20in (50cm) of fusible fleece
Scraps of plain cotton fabric in cream, blue, red, orange and yellow
8in (20cm) square of brown felt
4½in (11.5cm) square pieces of felt in cream, red, orange, white and beige
Chalk pencil or erasable marker
Six-stranded embroidery thread in red, orange, yellow, white and pink
Polyester toy stuffing
Pins
Dress-making scissors
General-purpose scissors
Quilter's square or ruler
Baking paper
Sewing machine
Sewing needle
Embroidery (crewel) needle
Thread to match fabric and felt
Iron and ironing board

1 For the bread slices, cut four bread shapes from cream fabric, using the outer line of the template. Cut four bread shapes from fusible fleece and two from craft foam, using the inner line of the template. Apply the pieces of fusible fleece to the wrong side of each fabric shape. With right sides together, stitch two fabric pieces around three sides, with a 1/4in (6mm) seam, leaving the bottom edge open. Do the same with the second pair of fabric pieces.

2 Snip into the seam allowance on the curved seams and turn right side out (see page 19). Insert a craft foam shape into each one, trimming it to fit if necessary.

3 Turn the raw edges to the inside and slipstitch folded edges together (see page 15) to close the gap. Cut four strips of brown felt to make the crusts. Each strip should measure 7½ x 3⁄8in (19 x 1cm). Sew two short ends of two of the strips together and wrap it around the edge of one of the bread slices. Oversew the edges of the felt to the fabric. Where the ends meet, trim off any excess and join them together.

4 For each cheese slice, cut two cheese shapes from yellow felt. For each ham slice, cut two ham shapes from pink felt and two fat shapes from white felt. Oversew the edges of the cheese pieces together with embroidery thread (see page 15); do the same with the ham, adding the two strips of fat to one edge. Add texture with lines of running stitch.

5 For each tomato slice, cut two of the round shapes from red felt, two of the inside shapes from orange and two cores from white. Place the red and orange shapes together and stitch the core in the centre using blanket stitch (see page 15). To suggest seeds, embroider detached chain stitches (see page 16) using yellow embroidery

thread and an embroidery needle. Place two of these prepared slices wrong sides together and stitch all around the edges using blanket stitch.

6 To make the crisp packet, you will need two pieces of blue fabric measuring 6½ x 5¼in (16.5 x 13cm) and small pieces of red fabric and yellow fabric. On the paper backing of a piece of bonding web, trace the symbols from page 149.

7 Fuse the bonding web with the circle shape to the red fabric and the banner shape to the yellow fabric (put a piece of baking paper on top to avoid getting glue on your iron). Cut out the shapes, peel off the backing paper and apply to the centre of one of the blue fabric pieces.

8 Place the two blue fabric rectangles with right sides together. Cut a piece of crinkle fabric the same size and place on top, then stitch sides and base with a 3⁄8in (1cm) seam. Clip corners and turn right side out (see page 19).

9 On the top (open) edge of the crisp packet, turn under raw edges twice to create a 3⁄8in (1cm) double hem. Stitch across the base of the packet 3⁄8in (1cm) from the bottom edge, to create a border. For the tortilla-chip packet, follow steps 6–9 using orange fabric for the bag, blue and yellow for the decoration, and the lightning-bolt shape for the symbol.

10 To create the crisps and tortilla chips, cut felt shapes using the template: two shapes for each crisp or chip. Pin pairs of shapes together and stitch all around the edges by machine or hand. For crinkle-cut crisps, add lines of stitching across the shape as shown.

11 To make the bag, use patterned fabric for the outside and plain fabric for the lining, and follow the instructions on page 130.

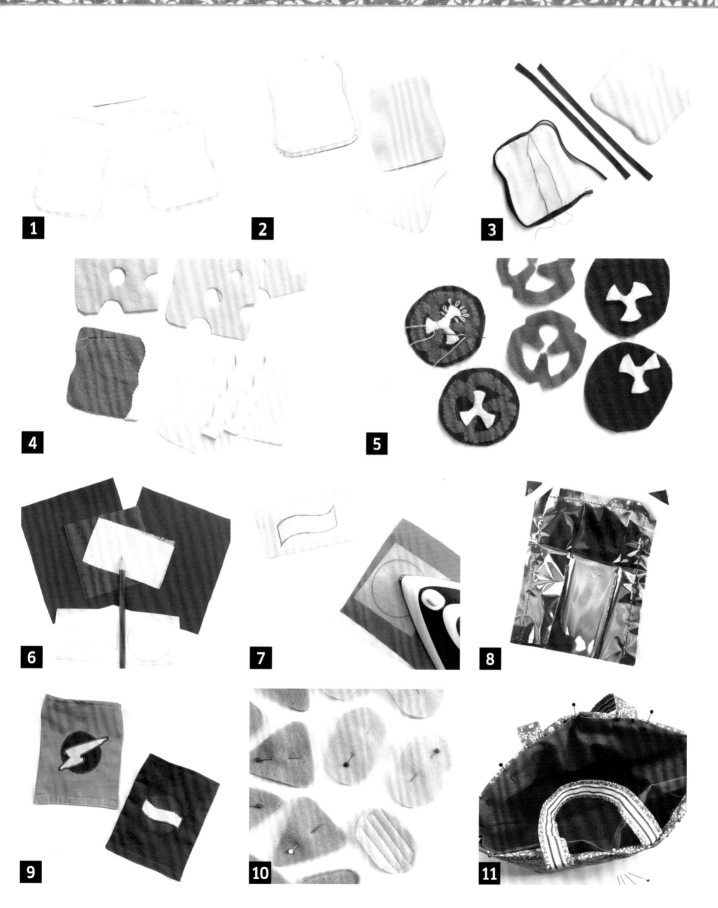

TOY BAG

Here is the perfect bag to transport toys from place to place, or to pack them away at the end of the day. This one is made with a pretty patterned fabric, but you will find another version in the picnic project on page 124.

Find the templates on page 149

You will need
1 fat quarter of printed cotton fabric for the bag
1 fat quarter of plain cotton fabric for the lining
20in (50cm) of fusible fleece
30in (76cm) of ½in (1.25cm)-wide cotton tape or ribbon
   for the bag handles
Pins
Dress-making scissors
General-purpose scissors
Plain paper for template
Sewing machine
Sewing needle
Thread to match fabric
Iron and ironing board

NOTE: The bag is interfaced with fusible fleece, which creates a soft, padded effect and helps to strengthen and reinforce the fabric.

Finished size is roughly:
8 x 5½ x 5in (20 x 14 x 12.75cm)

1 Fold both the main fabric and lining in half and press. Place on top of each other, with folded edges aligned. Copy the template on to paper and place this on the fabric with the marked edge on the fold. Pin in place, and cut out.

2 Use the template to cut out the fusible fleece exactly the same size as the fabric, then open it out and trim off ½in (1.25cm) all the way around. Place adhesive-side down on the wrong side of the main fabric and press with a hot iron to fuse in place (put a piece of paper on top of the fusible fleece to avoid getting glue on your iron).

3 Stitch the side seams of the bag with a ½in (1.25cm) seam allowance. Do the same with the lining.

4 Open out the corners and align the short edges and seams – this forms a gusset. Press, then stitch. Do the same with the lining.

5 For the handles, cut two strips, each measuring 13¾ x 2in (35 x 5cm), from the main fabric. Fold the long edges to the centre, as shown, and press.

6 To finish the handles, cut the length of ribbon or tape in half, then pin one piece down the centre of each handle, covering the raw edges of the fabric. Pin and stitch in place.

7 On the top edge of the bag, fold under ½in (1.25cm) to the inside, on the main fabric and the lining. Line up the seams, and pin the layers of fabric together.

8 Insert the ends of the handles between the bag and lining on either side, and pin in place. Then slipstitch the folded edge of the lining to the inside of the bag (see page 15).

9 Topstitch all around, approximately ⅛in (3mm) from the top edge (see page 17).

Tip

Instead of making a paper pattern, you could use a ruler and pencil or fabric marker to mark out the shape of the bag.

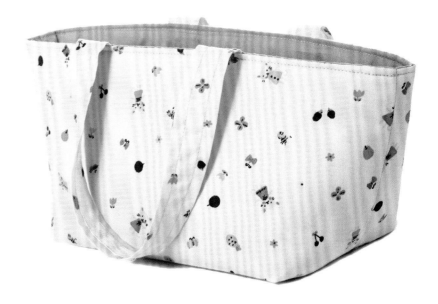

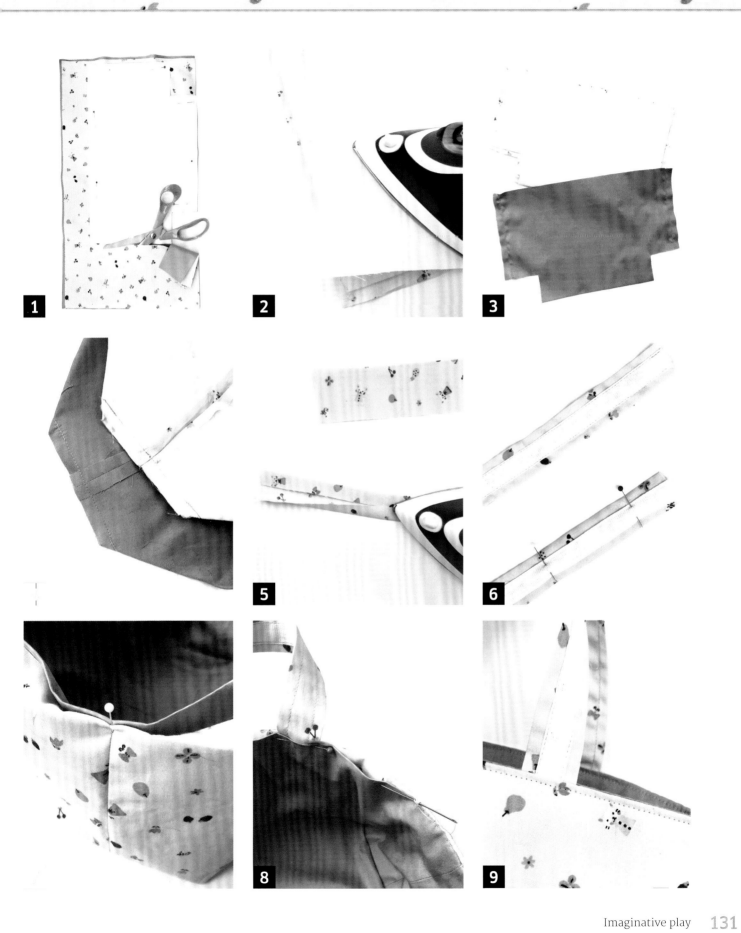

TEMPLATES

Templates that are shown at actual size can be
traced and cut out, or photocopied. For templates
that have been reduced in size, enlarge them on
an A3 photocopier to the percentage stated.

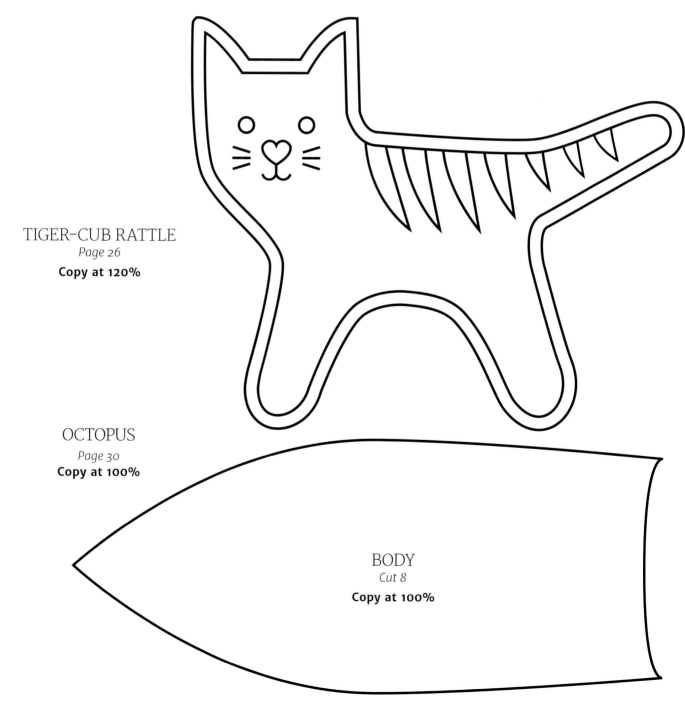

TIGER-CUB RATTLE
Page 26
Copy at 120%

OCTOPUS
Page 30
Copy at 100%

BODY
Cut 8
Copy at 100%

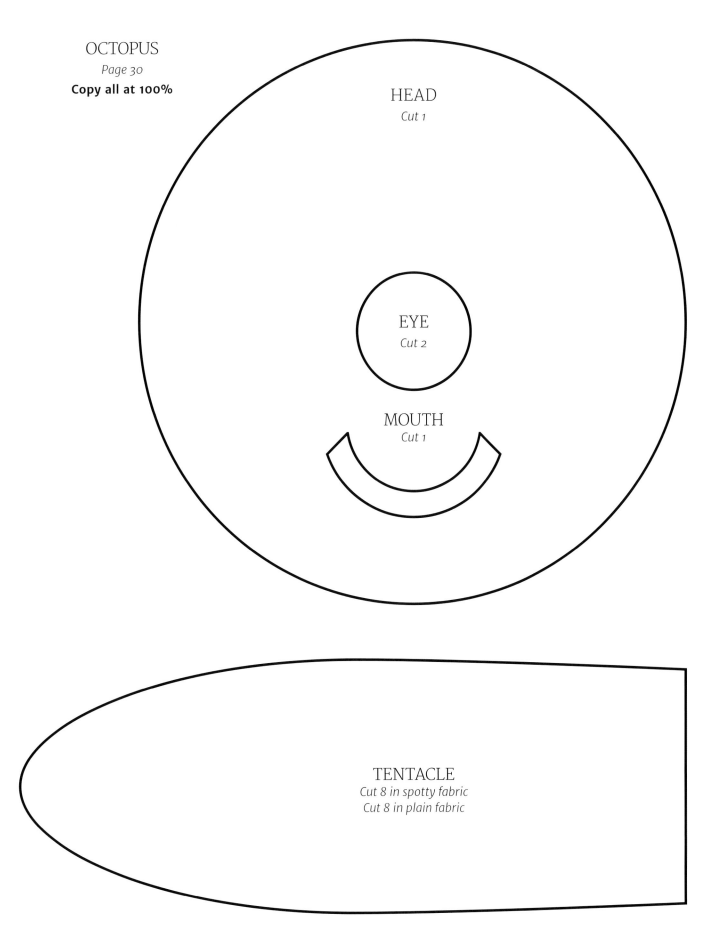

OCTOPUS
Page 30
Copy all at 100%

HEAD
Cut 1

EYE
Cut 2

MOUTH
Cut 1

TENTACLE
Cut 8 in spotty fabric
Cut 8 in plain fabric

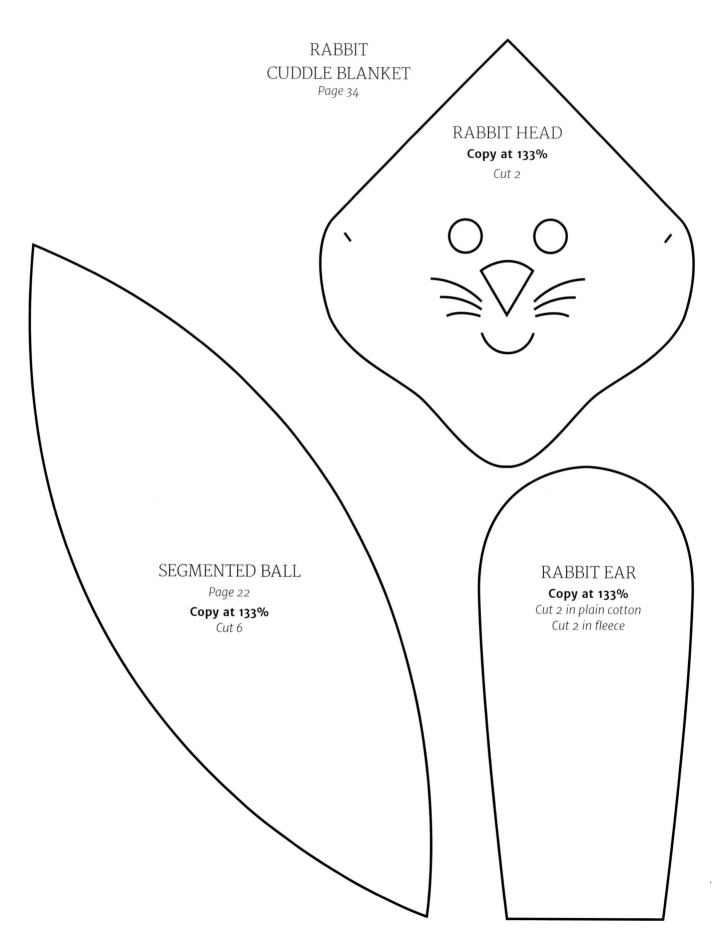

RABBIT
CUDDLE BLANKET
Page 34

RABBIT HEAD
Copy at 133%
Cut 2

SEGMENTED BALL
Page 22
Copy at 133%
Cut 6

RABBIT EAR
Copy at 133%
Cut 2 in plain cotton
Cut 2 in fleece

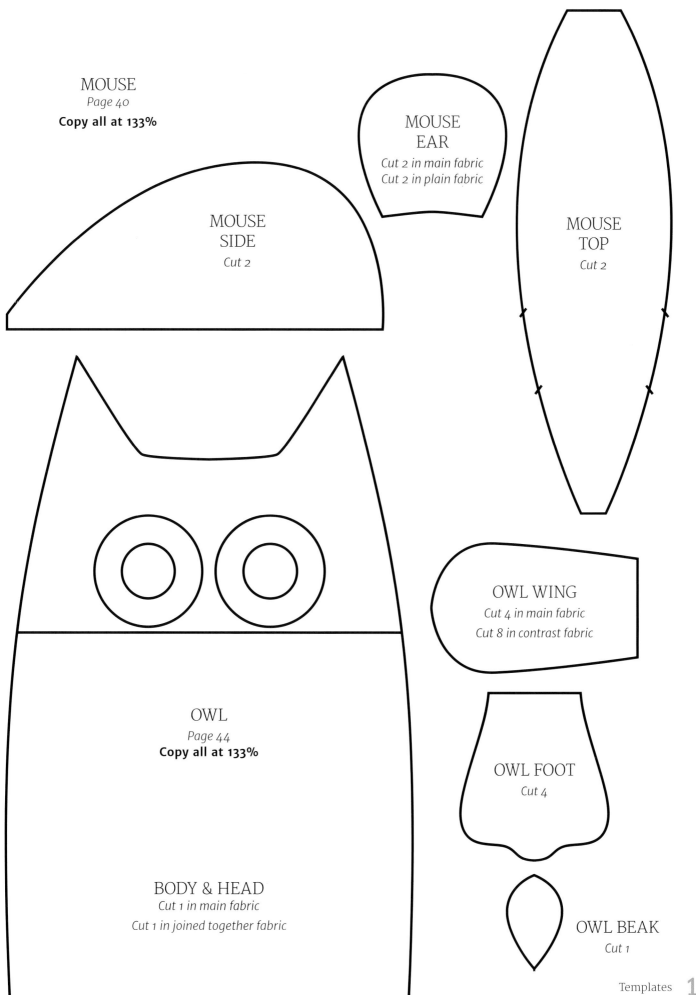

MOUSE
Page 40
Copy all at 133%

MOUSE
EAR
Cut 2 in main fabric
Cut 2 in plain fabric

MOUSE
SIDE
Cut 2

MOUSE
TOP
Cut 2

OWL WING
Cut 4 in main fabric
Cut 8 in contrast fabric

OWL
Page 44
Copy all at 133%

OWL FOOT
Cut 4

BODY & HEAD
Cut 1 in main fabric
Cut 1 in joined together fabric

OWL BEAK
Cut 1

TORTOISE
Page 48
Copy all at 100%

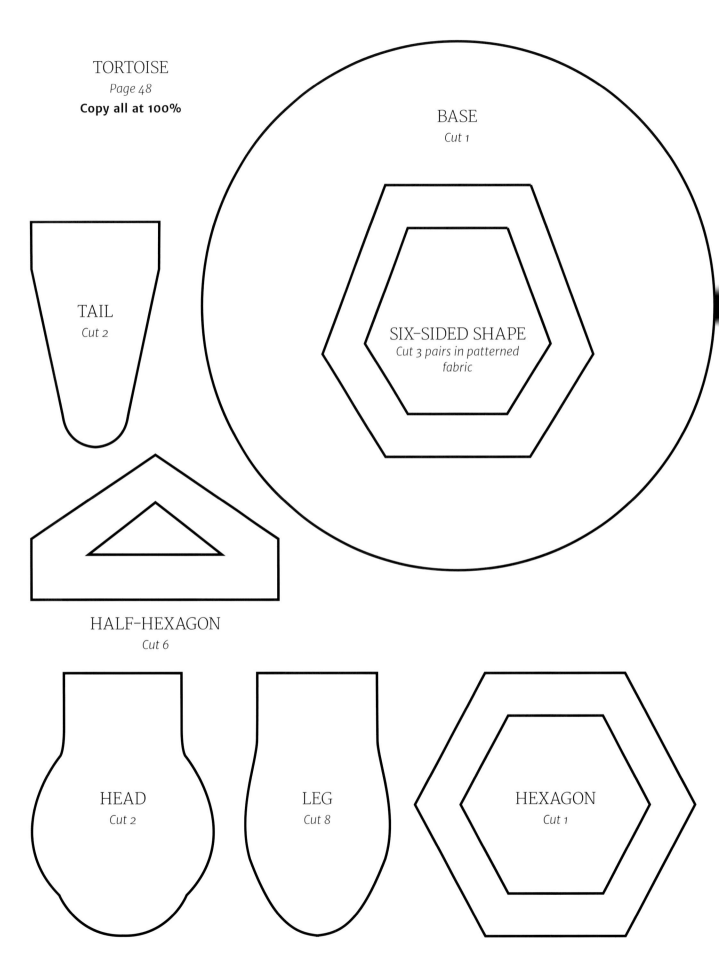

BASE
Cut 1

TAIL
Cut 2

SIX–SIDED SHAPE
Cut 3 pairs in patterned fabric

HALF–HEXAGON
Cut 6

HEAD
Cut 2

LEG
Cut 8

HEXAGON
Cut 1

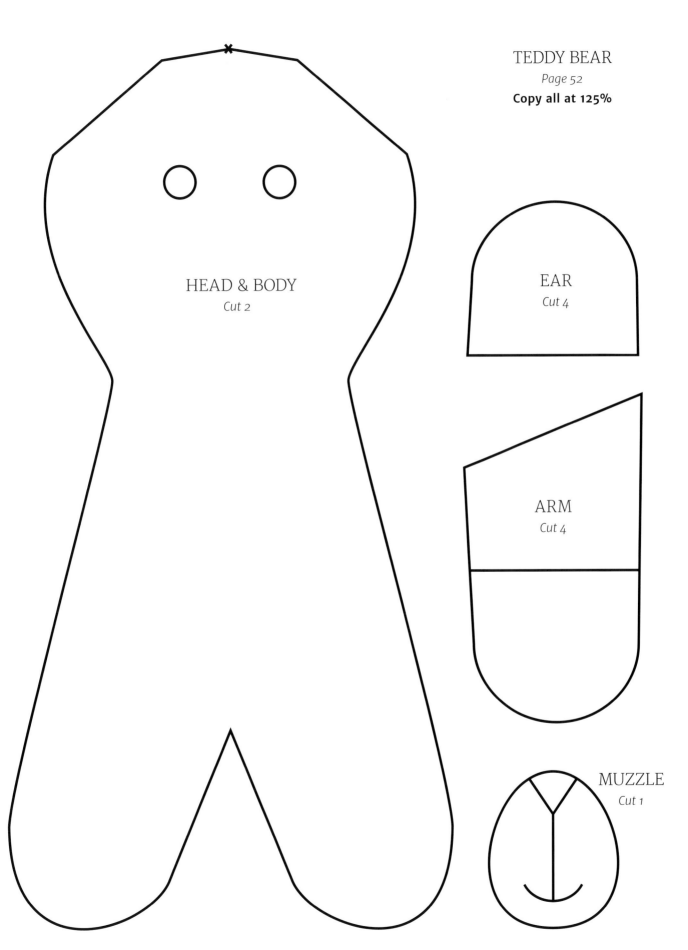

HEAD & BODY
Cut 2

TEDDY BEAR
Page 52
Copy all at 125%

EAR
Cut 4

ARM
Cut 4

MUZZLE
Cut 1

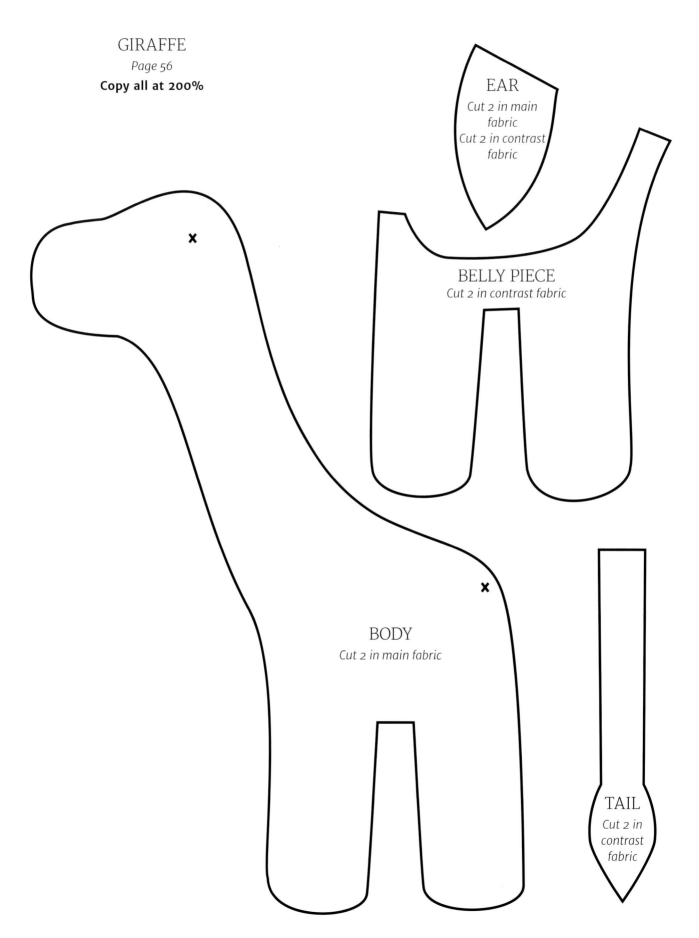

GIRAFFE

Page 56

Copy all at 200%

EAR

Cut 2 in main fabric

Cut 2 in contrast fabric

BELLY PIECE

Cut 2 in contrast fabric

BODY

Cut 2 in main fabric

TAIL

Cut 2 in contrast fabric

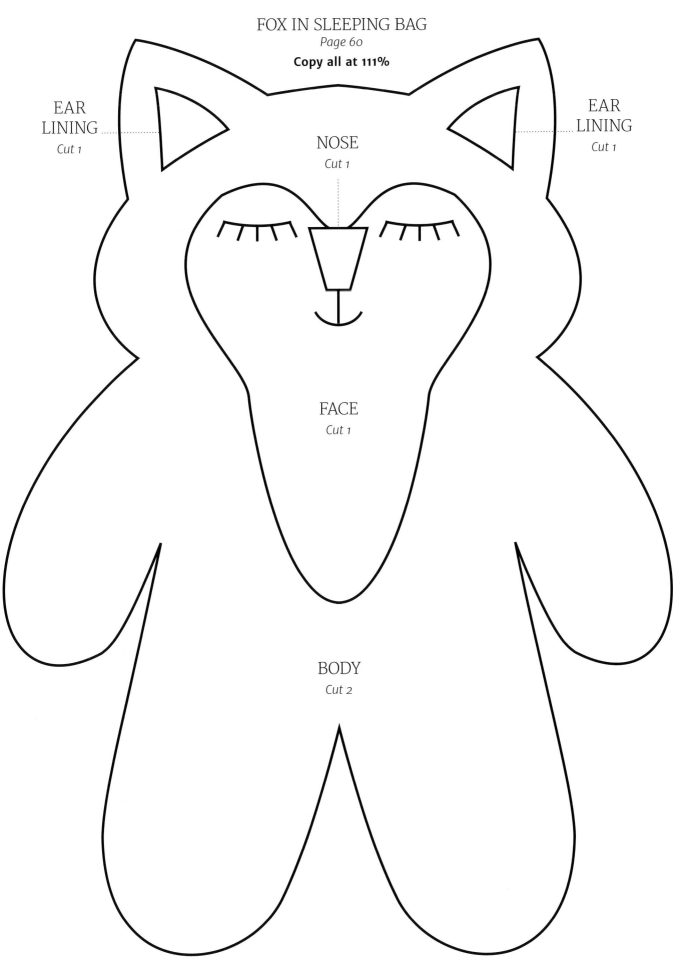

FOX IN SLEEPING BAG
Page 60
Copy all at 111%

EAR LINING
Cut 1

EAR LINING
Cut 1

NOSE
Cut 1

FACE
Cut 1

BODY
Cut 2

SKITTLES

Page 66
Copy all at 133%

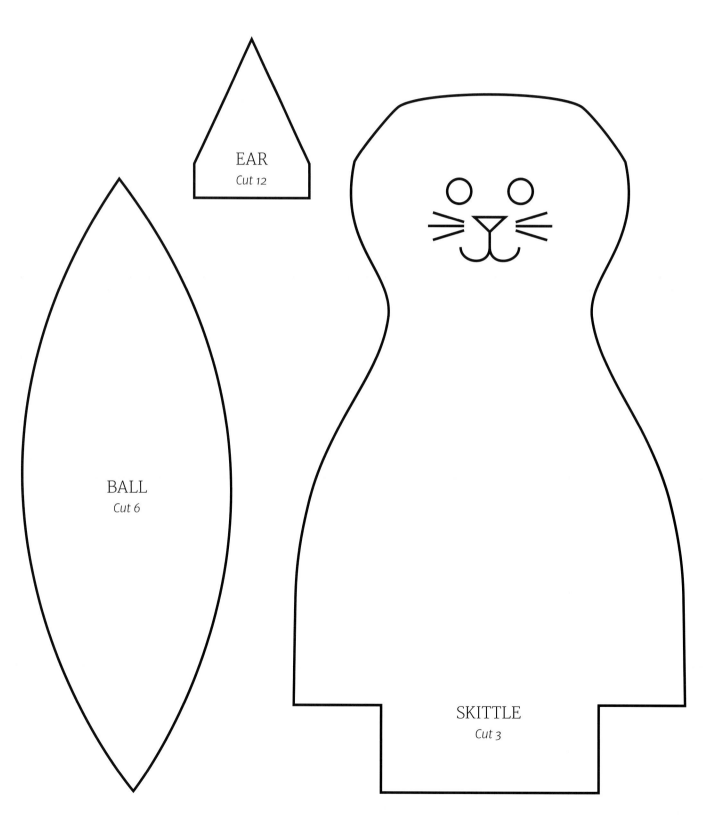

EAR
Cut 12

BALL
Cut 6

SKITTLE
Cut 3

FISHING SET
Page 70

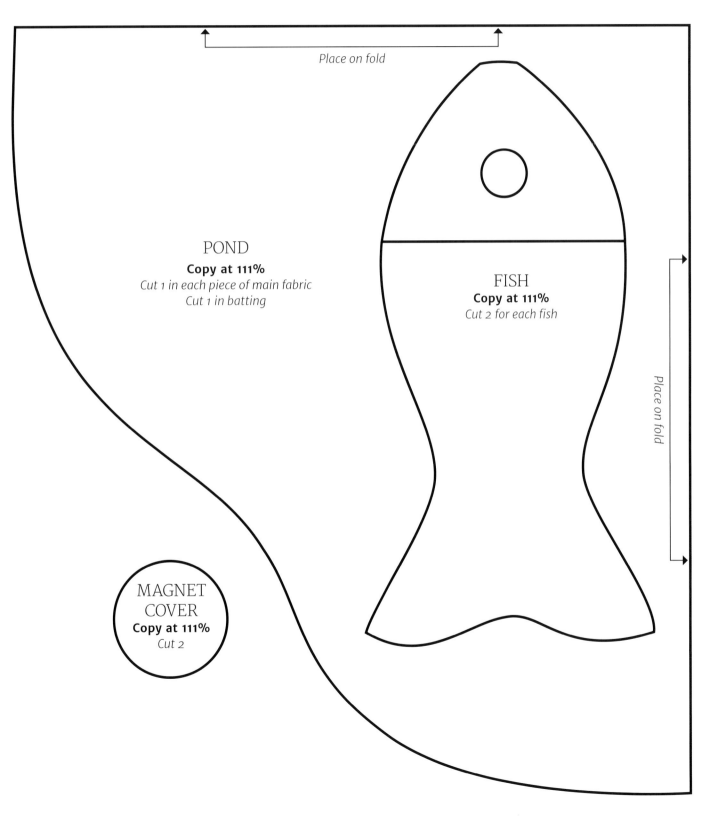

Place on fold

POND
Copy at 111%
Cut 1 in each piece of main fabric
Cut 1 in batting

FISH
Copy at 111%
Cut 2 for each fish

Place on fold

MAGNET
COVER
Copy at 111%
Cut 2

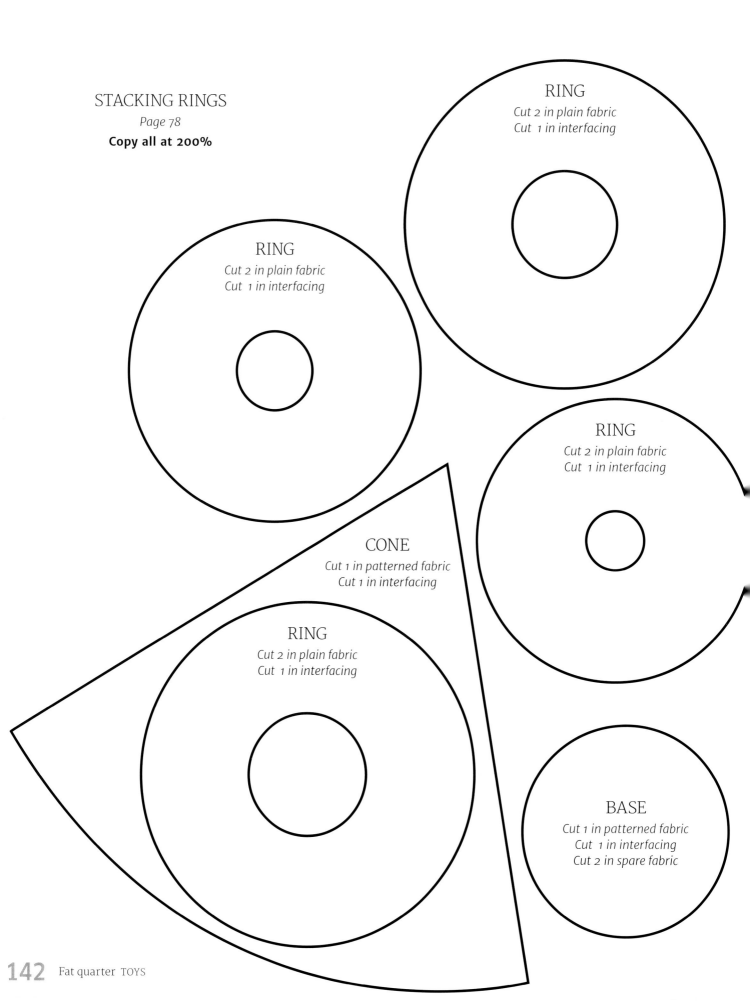

STACKING RINGS
Page 78
Copy all at 200%

RING
Cut 2 in plain fabric
Cut 1 in interfacing

RING
Cut 2 in plain fabric
Cut 1 in interfacing

RING
Cut 2 in plain fabric
Cut 1 in interfacing

CONE
Cut 1 in patterned fabric
Cut 1 in interfacing

RING
Cut 2 in plain fabric
Cut 1 in interfacing

BASE
Cut 1 in patterned fabric
Cut 1 in interfacing
Cut 2 in spare fabric

RING

Cut 2 in plain fabric
Cut 1 in interfacing

MEMORY GAME

Page 82

Copy at 100%

Cut 16 in each fat quarter
Cut 16 in fusible interfacing

Inner 'window'

Seam allowance

ABCD
EFGHIJKLM
NOPQRSTU
VWXYZ

ALPHABET IN A BAG

Page 88
Copy at 600%
Cut 1 in fabric and 1 in fusible bonding web for each letter

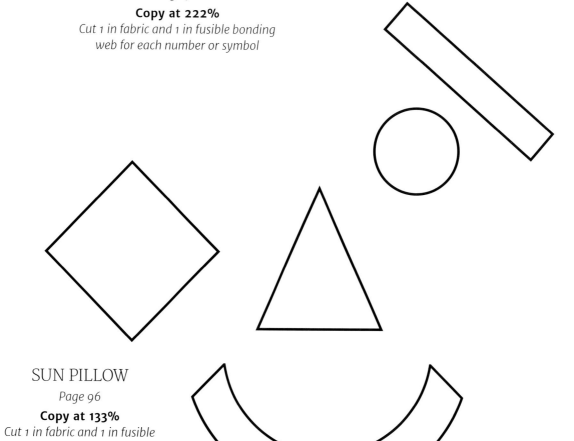

NUMBER CUBES

Page 92

Copy at 222%
*Cut 1 in fabric and 1 in fusible bonding
web for each number or symbol*

SUN PILLOW

Page 96

Copy at 133%
*Cut 1 in fabric and 1 in fusible
bonding web for each shape*

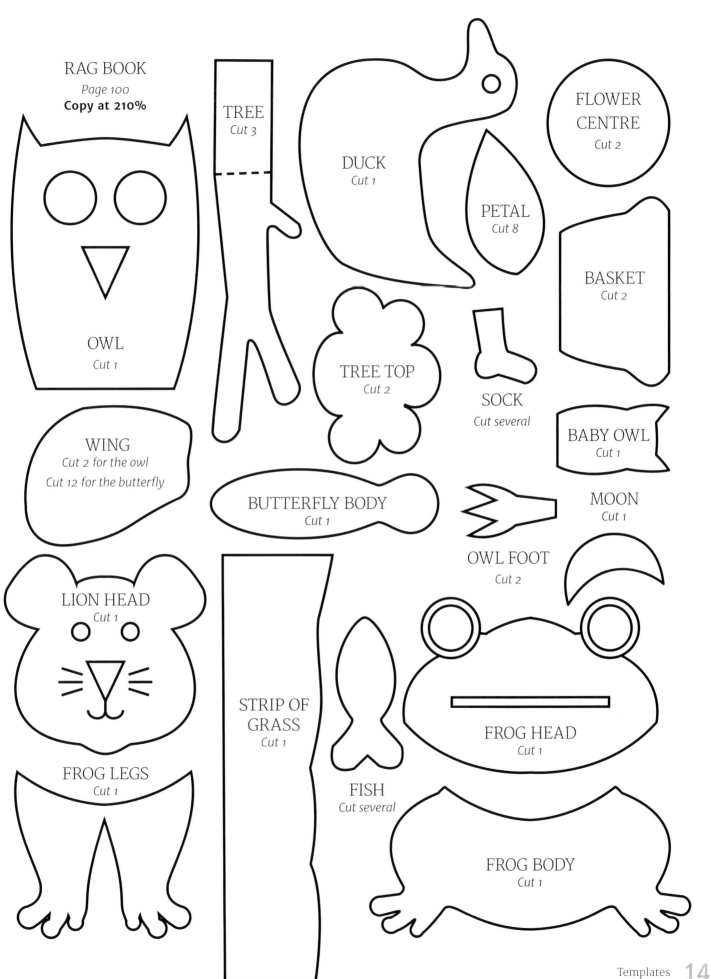

RAG BOOK
Page 100
Copy at 210%

OWL
Cut 1

TREE
Cut 3

DUCK
Cut 1

FLOWER CENTRE
Cut 2

PETAL
Cut 8

BASKET
Cut 2

WING
Cut 2 for the owl
Cut 12 for the butterfly

TREE TOP
Cut 2

SOCK
Cut several

BABY OWL
Cut 1

MOON
Cut 1

BUTTERFLY BODY
Cut 1

OWL FOOT
Cut 2

LION HEAD
Cut 1

STRIP OF GRASS
Cut 1

FISH
Cut several

FROG HEAD
Cut 1

FROG LEGS
Cut 1

FROG BODY
Cut 1

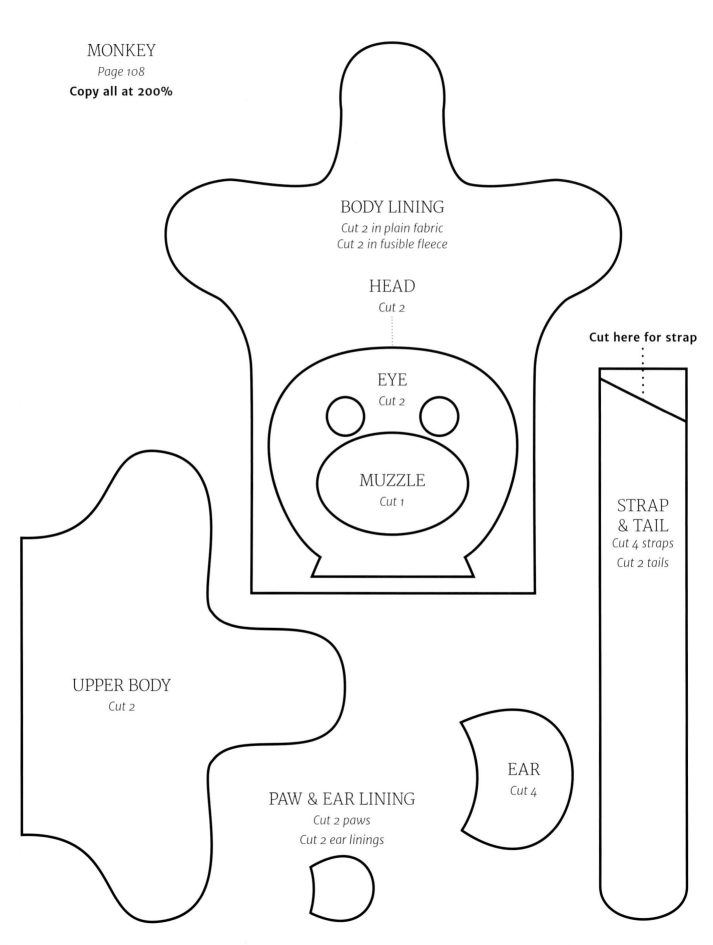

MONKEY
Page 108
Copy all at 200%

BODY LINING
Cut 2 in plain fabric
Cut 2 in fusible fleece

HEAD
Cut 2

EYE
Cut 2

MUZZLE
Cut 1

Cut here for strap

STRAP
& TAIL
Cut 4 straps
Cut 2 tails

UPPER BODY
Cut 2

EAR
Cut 4

PAW & EAR LINING
Cut 2 paws
Cut 2 ear linings

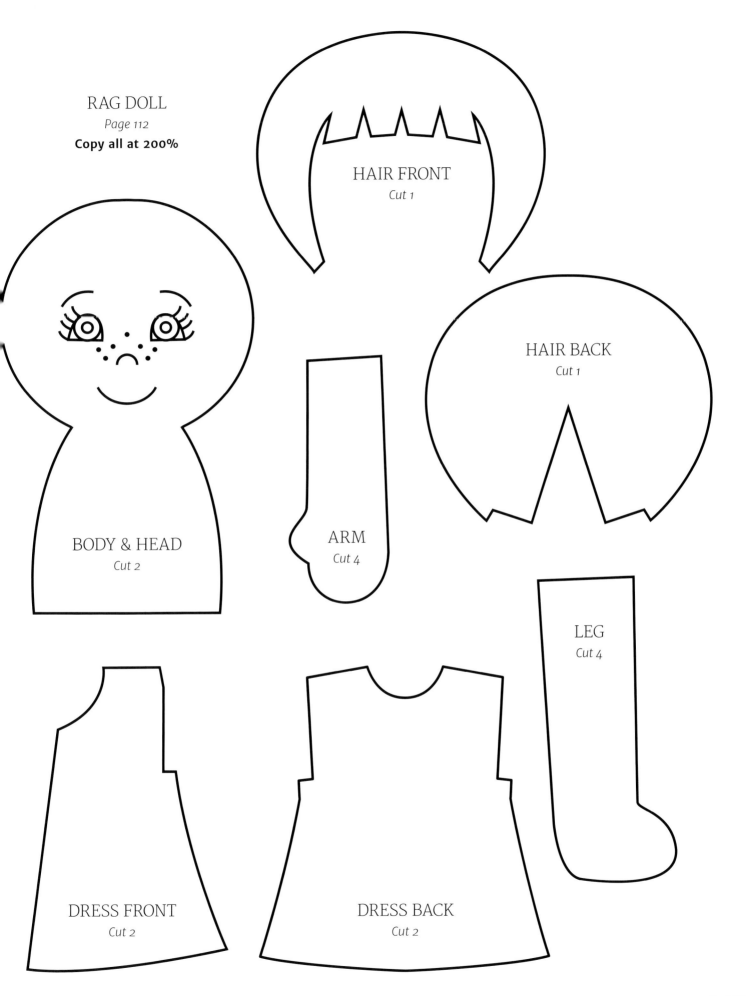

RAG DOLL

Page 112

Copy all at 200%

HAIR FRONT
Cut 1

HAIR BACK
Cut 1

BODY & HEAD
Cut 2

ARM
Cut 4

LEG
Cut 4

DRESS FRONT
Cut 2

DRESS BACK
Cut 2

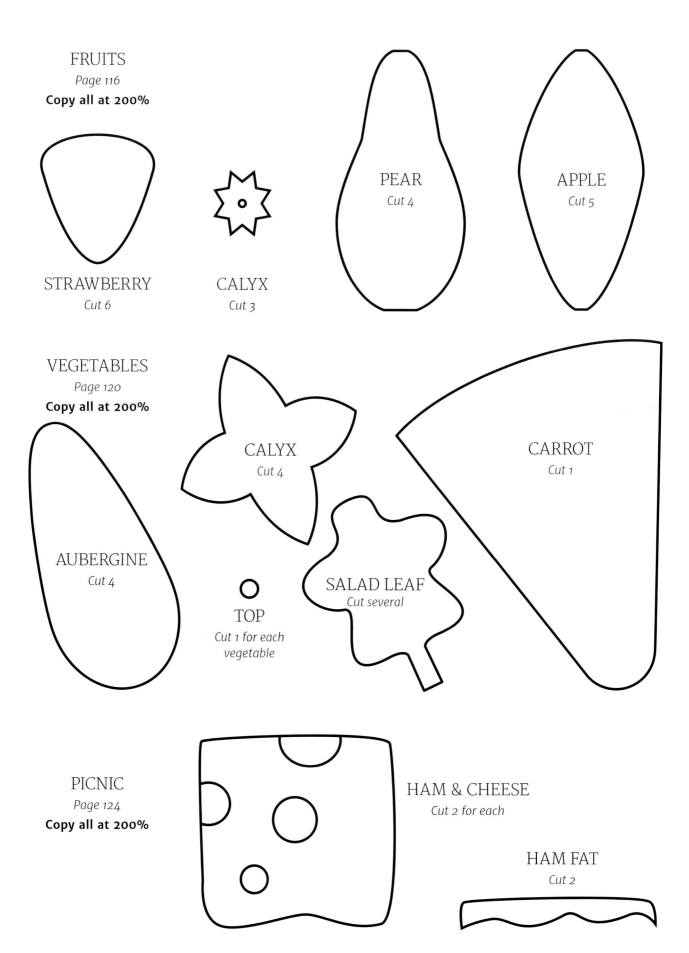

FRUITS
Page 116
Copy all at 200%

STRAWBERRY
Cut 6

CALYX
Cut 3

PEAR
Cut 4

APPLE
Cut 5

VEGETABLES
Page 120
Copy all at 200%

CALYX
Cut 4

CARROT
Cut 1

AUBERGINE
Cut 4

TOP
Cut 1 for each
vegetable

SALAD LEAF
Cut several

PICNIC
Page 124
Copy all at 200%

HAM & CHEESE
Cut 2 for each

HAM FAT
Cut 2

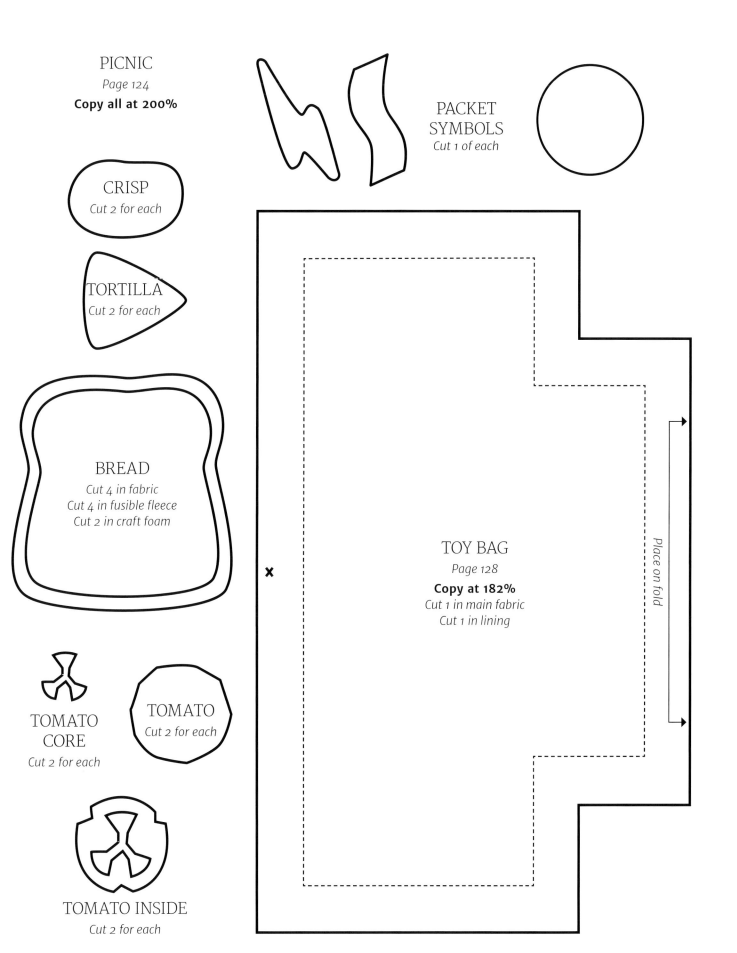

PICNIC

Page 124

Copy all at 200%

CRISP

Cut 2 for each

TORTILLA

Cut 2 for each

BREAD

Cut 4 in fabric
Cut 4 in fusible fleece
Cut 2 in craft foam

TOMATO
CORE

Cut 2 for each

TOMATO

Cut 2 for each

TOMATO INSIDE

Cut 2 for each

PACKET
SYMBOLS

Cut 1 of each

TOY BAG

Page 128

Copy at 182%
Cut 1 in main fabric
Cut 1 in lining

Place on fold

✕

RESOURCES

Cotton fabrics, fat quarters
www.craftcotton.com
www.fabricland.co.uk

Dimple fleece fabric, fusible interfacing and fleece
www.empressmills.co.uk
www.plushaddict.co.uk

Felt
www.trouva.com
www.woolfeltcompany.co.uk

Rattles, bells, squeakers, jingles, foam cubes and crinkle material
www.tactiletreasures
www.fredaldous.co.uk

General haberdashery
www.sewandso.co.uk
www.sewing-online.com

Embroidery threads, hoops and quilter's square
www.cottonpatch.co.uk
www.sewessential.co.uk

Sewing machines and accessories
www.jaycotts.co.uk
www.sewingmachines.co.uk

ACKNOWLEDGEMENTS

Many thanks to Jonathan Bailey for asking me to write this book; to Sara Harper for her patience and organizational skills; to Cath Senker for editing the text so meticulously; to Gilda Pacitti and her team for designing the book; to Neal Grundy for photographing the finished items; and to Wayne Blades for styling the photographs. Thanks also to my mother and grandmothers for teaching me to sew in the first place; to my daughter Lillie for her opinions and feedback as the projects were being made; and to Violeta and Scarlet for testing the finished toys.

GMC Publications would like to thank Amelia and William Stevens and Ivy Motley for modelling; Anna Stevens for providing the location for the shoot; and Wayne Blades for the photography styling.

PICTURE CREDITS

Cover illustrations: Ohn Mar/Shutterstock/; page 24: nattha99/Shutterstock; page 28: nnattalli/Shutterstock.

INDEX

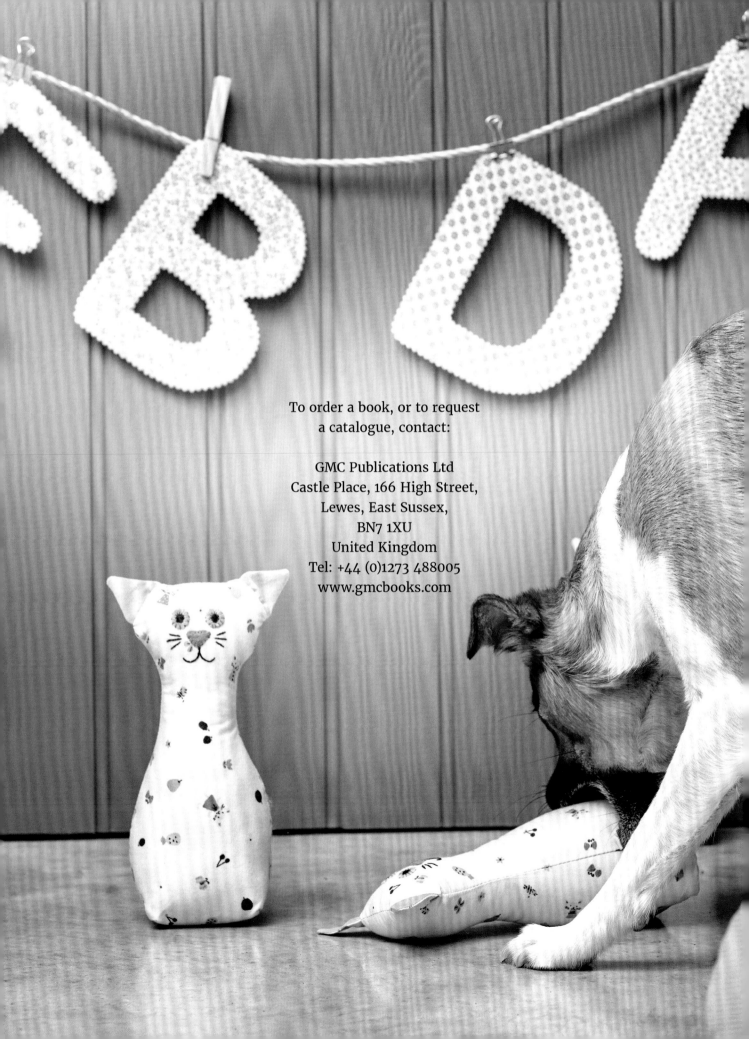

To order a book, or to request
a catalogue, contact:

GMC Publications Ltd
Castle Place, 166 High Street,
Lewes, East Sussex,
BN7 1XU
United Kingdom
Tel: +44 (0)1273 488005
www.gmcbooks.com